CARL HENRY

AT HIS BEST

CARL HENRY

AT HIS BEST

A
Lifetime
of
Quotable
Thoughts

Foreword by Charles Colson

MULTNOMAH

Portland, Oregon 97266

Cover design by Durand Demlow
Edited by Steve Halliday and Al Janssen

CARL HENRY AT HIS BEST
© 1989 by Carl F. H. Henry
Published by Multnomah Press
Portland, Oregon 97266

Multnomah Press is a ministry of Multnomah School of the Bible,
8435 N.E. Glisan Street, Portland, Oregon 97220.

Printed in the United States of America

Library of Congress Cataloging-in-Publication Data

Henry, Carl Ferdinand Howard, 1913-
    Carl Henry at his best : a lifetime of quotable thoughts / Carl F. H.
Henry.
      p.   cm.
    "Books by Carl F. H. Henry": p.
    ISBN 0-88070-355-5
    1. Henry, Carl Ferdinand Howard, 1913- —Quotations.   I. Title.
BR1643.H47A25   1990
230'.044—dc20   90-32010
                                                CIP

90 91 92 93 94 95 96 97 98 99 - 10 9 8 7 6 5 4 3 2 1

CONTENTS

CONTENTS

ABBREVIATIONS

All quotations in this book are followed by letter and number codes that indicate the source from which the extract is taken. Quotes from books also include the original page number on which the extract appears. For example:

> The soul of modern man has been sucked dry by temporary concerns that eclipse the eternal world. (NSF, 61)

The letters NSF indicate the quotation is taken from *New Strides of Faith*, and the number 61 indicates that the extract is found on page 61 of that work.

Below is an alphabetical list of the sources used in this collection, followed by the code used to identify the work in this book.

Books by Carl F. H. Henry

Aspects of Christian Social Ethics. Grand Rapids, Mich.: William B. Eerdmans, 1964. (ACSE)

Christian Countermoves in a Decadent Culture. Portland, Ore.: Multnomah, 1986. (CCDC)

The Christian Mindset in a Secular Society. Portland, Ore.: Multnomah, 1985. (CMSS)

Christian Personal Ethics. Grand Rapids, Mich.: Baker Book House, 1957. Used by permission. (CPE)

Confessions of a Theologian. Waco, Tex.: Word, 1986. Used by permission. (COT)

Conversations with Carl Henry: Christianity for Today. Lewiston, N.Y.: Edwin Mellen, 1986. (CCH)

A Doorway to Heaven. Grand Rapids, Mich.: Zondervan, 1941. (DTH)

The Drift of Western Thought. Grand Rapids, Mich.: William B. Eerdmans, 1951. (DWT)

Evangelical Responsibility in Contemporary Theology. Grand Rapids, Mich.: William B. Eerdmans, 1957. (ERCT)

Evangelicals at the Brink of Crisis. Waco, Tex.: Word, 1967. (EBC)

Evangelicals in Search of Identity. Waco, Tex.: Word, 1976. (ESI)

Faith at the Frontiers. Chicago: Moody Press, 1969. (FAF)

Fifty Years of Protestant Theology. Rocky Mount, N.C.: Wilde & Associates, 1950. (FYPT)

Frontiers in Modern Theology. Chicago: Moody Press, 1966. (FMT)

Giving a Reason for Our Hope. Rocky Mount, N.C.: Wilde & Associates, 1949. (GROH)

Glimpses of a Sacred Land. Rocky Mount, N.C.: Wilde & Associates, 1953. (GSL)

God, Revelation and Authority. Vols. I-II, 1976; Vols. III-IV 1979; Vol. V, 1982; Vol. VI, 1983. Waco, Tex.: Word. Used by permission. (GRA)

The God Who Shows Himself. Waco, Tex.: Word, 1966. (GWSH)

New Strides of Faith. Chicago: Moody Press, 1972. (NSF)

Notes on the Doctrine of God. Rocky Mount, N.C.: Wilde & Associates, 1949. (NDG)

Personal Idealism and Strong's Theology. Van Kampen, 1951. (PIST)

A Plea for Evangelical Demonstration. Grand Rapids, Mich.: Baker Book House, 1971. Used by permission. (PED)

The Protestant Dilemma. Grand Rapids, Mich.: William B. Eerdmans, 1949. (PD)

Remaking the Modern Mind. Grand Rapids, Mich.: William B. Eerdmans, 1948. (RMM)

Successful Church Publicity. Grand Rapids, Mich.: Zondervan, 1942. (SCP)

Twilight of a Great Civilization. Westchester, Ill.: Crossway Books, 1988. Used by permission. (TGC)

The Uneasy Conscience of Modern Fundamentalism. Grand Rapids, Mich.: William B. Eerdmans, 1948. (UCMF)

Magazine and Newspaper Articles

Newby, James R., ed., *Between Peril and Promise*. (BPP)
"Morals and Politics," *Christian Herald*. (CH)
"Concerns and Considerations," *Christianity Today*. (CT)
"Why We Need Christian Think Tanks," *Christianity Today*. (CT2)
"Shall We Fear God?," *Cornerstone*. (C)
"The House Divided," *Eternity*. (E)
"The Making of a Christian Mind," *Eternity*. (E2)
"Humanism, Christianity Will Clash," *His People*. (HP)
"Christians in Politics," *Light*. (L)
"Why Christians Differ Politically," *Presbyterian Journal*. (PJ)
"Talking with Carl Henry," *Reformed Journal*. (RJ)
"Worldview of a Theologian," *Religious Broadcasting*. (RB)
"Evangelicals' Influence Continues Its Upsurge," *Sacramento Bee*. (SB)
"Evangelical Identity," *Sojourners*. (S)
"The Battle for the Bible," *Trinity Scribe*. (TS)
"Christian-Secular Battle Lines," *Vancouver Province*. (VP)
"Faith, Science Can Co-Exist," *Washington Star*. (WS3)
"Our Planet's in Peril," *Washington Star*. (WS2)
"Our Planet's in Trouble," *Washington Star*. (WS)
"Easter: Decisive for the Christian Faith," *Washington Times*. (WT)
"The Resurrection Is What Life Is All About," *Washington Times*. (WT2)
"Wheaton and the Evangelicals," *Wheaton Record*. (WR)

Speeches

Opening address to 1966 World Congress on Evangelism, Berlin. (WCE)

FOREWORD

Of what use, some might wonder, is a collection of quotations from a contemporary theologian?

Indeed, I might have expressed such sentiments myself, were it not for the particular theologian whose ideas are captured here, or for my own indebtness to one of the quotations as a watershed in my own journey of faith and ministry.

I was a fairly new believer, recently released from prison and trying to put together a ministry bringing the gospel to men and women in the penal system. One day I picked up a copy of the *Washington Star* that included an interview with Dr. Carl F. H. Henry. I was familiar with the name, but I did not at the time realize the tremendous significance of the man. Nor could I have guessed how that one interview would affect my life in Christ.

Then I read Henry's grand quote: "The intellectual decision most urgently facing humanity in our time is whether to acknowledge or disown Jesus Christ as the hope of the world and whether Christian values are to be the arbiter of human civilization in the present instead of only in the final judgment of men and nations."

Those words hit me powerfully, opening my eyes to the realization that God rules over history, that there is a continuing conflict between our Christian values and modern culture, and that the ultimate issue facing our society is whether or not to submit to Christ's rule in the present or face the judgment to come.

Enlivened by Dr. Henry's words, I began to see that Christianity was more than just being born again and growing spiritually. It was more than escaping judgment and being assured of eternal life. Being a Christian meant I had a duty to make a difference in the world, to bring Christian truth to bear on the issues of my day, to challenge the false suppositions of secular life, to make a bold and majestic witness to the holy commandments of God.

I wrote down that quotation and tucked it in the back of my Bible as a constant reminder of the social imperatives of the gospel and of every Christian's duty to incarnate and declare God's justice and righteousness in a sinful and dying world.

There are hundreds of other, equally cogent declarations and statements in the vast corpus of Carl Henry's theological output, many of which you will find in the pages that follow. Since the 1940s Carl Henry has been the foremost spokesman and one of the most diligent and effective laborers on behalf of evangelical Christianity. His books, editorials, lectures, and contributions to publications scholarly and popular, as well as his service on boards and groups within evangelical circles, have made him the dominant figure in what has become the largest and fastest growing movement of contemporary Christianity in the world today.

But beyond these, Carl Henry as a man embodies the things he has taught and believed.

It was not long after I read Carl Henry's life-changing words that I sought him out. He graciously invited me to lunch. We sat around the dining room table in his modest Arlington, Virginia, home, enjoying lunch and fellowship for two hours. Carl's wife, Helga, a strong and informed partner to him as well as a gracious hostess, joined us.

What impressed me most during that time was that this man of extraordinary intellect and vast reputation was at the same time so genuinely humble. I have known some brilliant people in my life—college professors of national renown, world leaders, academics, Nobel Prize winners. Carl Henry is a match for any of them intellectually, but he is totally unlike them in his humility.

We became friends, and I drank deeply at the fount of Carl Henry's teaching. But over the years I discovered that he was more than just a great teacher. He is a helper and encourager with a pastor's heart. From time to time I would receive personal notes from Carl in which he would share clippings or articles he thought I could use, or explicated ideas for some speech or editorial.

His work has continued to shape my Christian life and ministry to this day. Henry's most prophetic warnings to western culture are compiled in his book *Twilight of a Great Civilization*. Those sobering messages inspired much of my own writings, including *Against the Night*, which I dedicated to Dr. Henry.

Although Carl is one of the busiest men I know, maintaining a schedule that would exhaust someone half his age, he is never too busy to help a friend. When I was doing the final drafts of *Kingdoms In Conflict*, I sent a copy to him and asked if he would check it over theologically, just one quick reading. I told him I needed it fairly soon, but that I recognized the pressures on him and could he possibly have it back to me, in say, thirty days?

To my astonishment, the manuscript was returned the next day by messenger. Carl explained in a cover note that he was about to embark on an extended trip and thought he'd better get it done before he left. So he stayed up most of the night writing comments on the manuscript.

This was no isolated instance; this desire to help others is ingrained in the man's character. A friend accompanied Carl Henry on a trip through Romania in 1988, and described his ministry as amazing. Everywhere he went he was prepared to speak. The size of the group didn't matter. It strikes me as remarkable to think of this towering theologian speaking to small groups of Christians clustered in homes throughout Romania. Yet I'm certain that to Carl Henry there would be nothing remarkable in this whatsoever. As the media icons of the evangelical world fall and flounder around us, it is heartening to know that there are people like this. Carl Henry is surely one of God's genuine articles.

I suspect that it is this personal genuineness, as much as any of his writings or other labors, that has made him the giant that he is. When the history of the evangelical movement is finally written, Carl Henry will emerge as its dominant figure.

And not without good cause. Not only have his theological and popular writings helped to define and shape the evangelical faith between the Scylla and Charybdis of fundamentalism and neo-orthodoxy, but he has played a leadership role in the key institutions of that movement as well. Beginning with his formative role in the National Association of Evangelicals in 1943 and continuing through his role in the founding of Fuller Theological Seminary (1947) and *Christianity Today* (1956), Carl Henry has made major contributions to the creation of a vibrant and dynamic evangelical theology. He has given encouragement and guidance to Billy Graham, and he has served as the Chairman of the Berlin Congress on World Evangelization (1966). He was in the forefront of those who, in 1973, sought to bring more social relevance to the evangelical faith through the Chicago Declaration of Evangelical Social Concern. He has also provided stimulation and encouragement to the Evangelical Theological Society since its founding in 1949.

Through it all, Carl Henry has maintained a widespread ministry of preaching and lecturing. He has spoken to groups on every major evangelical college campus, at secular universities throughout the land, in hundreds of churches, and in dozens of countries. And the good news for the Christian world is that he shows no signs of slowing down.

Henry's magnum opus, *God, Revelation, and Authority*, represents his theological thinking at its best: a vast compendium of biblical insight, theological acumen, philosophical awareness, apologetical expertise, and pastoral concern. The quotations in this book from that six-volume masterpiece are on there own worth the price of admission.

The quotations that follow represent the intellectual and spiritual struggles of a man, a movement, and a generation. Certain individuals, by the dominance of their lives over a given space of time, give definition to the eras in which they live and become identified as the personal embodiments of the trials and triumphs of their generation. One thinks of Athanasius and the Arian controversy of the fourth century; of Augustine and the triumph of Christianity over pagan Rome; of Calvin and Luther and the struggle to reform the church in sixteenth-century Europe; of Whitefield and Edwards and the revivals of the colonial era; of Wilberforce and Shaftesbury and the triumphs of nineteenth-century evangelical social concern; and of Taylor, Livingstone, Studd, Judson, Carmichael, and the greatest outbreak of world missions in church history.

Carl Henry is such a man. It would be fair to say that he midwifed, nurtured, watched over, raised, and, where necessary, disciplined the revitalized evangelicalism of the late twentieth century to its present state of budding maturity. It remains to be seen whether that movement—and we of this generation of evangelicals—will be able to live up to the vision and conviction of the statement that so affected me as a new Christian, or to the humility and energy of the man who brought that statement to life. With this book before us as a stimulus and reminder, we may yet manage to prevail against the night in the darkening twilight of a great civilization.

Charles W. Colson

ABSOLUTES

Any nation that ignores moral absolutes is in danger of marching off the map. (SB)

The soul of modern man has been sucked dry by temporary concerns that eclipse the eternal world. (NSF, 61)

No nation has an advance guarantee of perpetuity if it trades moral absolutes for so-called political prudence. (CCDC, 32)

Despite the personal religious faith of many of the nation's political leaders, despite the public virtues still cherished by the grassroots citizenry, and despite the emphasis on representative pluralism which is declared to reflect national concerns comprehensively, the values traditionally considered normative in American society are now flouted with impunity in many of the nation's influential and prestigious educational institutions, in the mass media, and even by some political leaders. (CMSS, 130)

I think it's fair to say that representatives of the press are not at home in a discussion of moral absolutes. (HP)

Vast multitudes think they escape measurement by an absolute simply because they affirm that no absolute exists and follow their gut-instincts. Many influential educators, under whom the young study, have no serious interest in revealed religion and lack effective sanctions to curtail the seething corruption of our age. (CH)

The ideals that lifted the West above ancient paganism had their deepest source and support in the self-revealed God who was and is for Christians the *summum bonum* or supreme good. (CCDC, 9)

Any reader of the Bible will recognize at once how ancient, and not at all distinctively modern, is this revolt against spiritual and moral absolutes. The emphasis on human autonomy is pre-"secular" and pre-"modern" and carries us all the way back to Eden. (GRA IV, 11)

Our generation largely settles for grime when it could reach for glory; it is indifferent to spiritual values. (WS)

All the great value-words, like liberty, truth, justice and the good, are loaded today with conflicting and even contradictory meanings. But counterfeits always presuppose an authentic original. (WT)

The loss of biblical virtues and vitalities is the occasion of the moral confusion of our age, besieged as it now is by sensate, scientific, and sexual priorities. (CCDC, 28)

No life in community is possible without a widely shared consensus on what is lawful. . . . Many observers argue, however, that a firm social consensus no longer exists. (CMSS, 119)

Without shared values, democracy is on the move to anarchy. (CCDC, 31)

Despite national consensus on the urgent need for shared values, less and less agreement exists on which values to champion and why. (TGC, 169)

More than fifty years ago, when secular universities forsook God as the integrating factor in learning, they turned instead to "shared" values—only to discover that values divorced from metaphysical anchorage cannot escape a relativizing fate. (TGC, 88)

Those who deplore as intellectual chauvinism any claim to the finality of certain truths and to the superiority of certain values have no logical option but to concede that rape, terrorism and murder may be as right as their opposites, or that the value of a camel may be as great as that of a man. (GRA V, 394)

Are you yourself debilitated by the shoddy secular values of our time? (TGC, 43)

You can be part of a strategic alliance who take God and moral absolutes and divine truth seriously; you can lead in the renewing of our crumbling society. The cause of justice and peace in society is a noble one, and evangelicals should be in the forefront of it. (CCDC, 143)

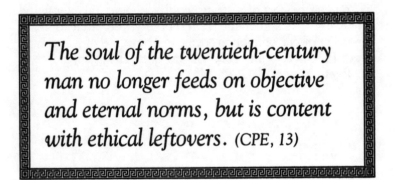

The soul of the twentieth-century man no longer feeds on objective and eternal norms, but is content with ethical leftovers. (CPE, 13)

AMERICA

Speaking for a national morality movement, an evangelical leader recently remarked: "The United States has turned away from God. It mocks God. It worships a twentieth-century Baal. . . . incarnated in sensuality, material goods, and immorality of every kind". . . . Yet only a few years ago we were told that a new evangelical awakening had dawned in America; this very decade, it was said, is the decade of the evangelicals. (CMSS, 9)

Our nation increasingly trips the worst ratings on God's Richter scale of fully deserved moral judgment. (TGC, 41)

God isn't bullish either on the Communist world or on the free world or on present-day America. (WS2)

We Americans are not God's covenant people. America has, in any event, no biblical guarantee of perpetuity. (CH)

If our nation has a real future, political leaders too will have an eye on God in his revelation and declared purposes as much as on the pollsters and their prognostications. (WS)

American culture seems to be sinking toward sunset. I do not, like some, call America the epicenter of evil in the world. But we have fallen far from lofty ideals for which this land came into being. Our country seems more and more to act out of traditional character. To be sure, there is a godly remnant—not simply a tiny band but a goodly number—for which we may be grateful. But it is surely not America at her best when we chart the massacre of a million unborn children a year, the flight from the monogamous family, two and a half million persons trapped in illegal drugs and alcohol, the normalizing of deviant sexual behavior, the proliferation of AIDS. (TGC, 40)

It is true that God in sovereign mercy often spares a nation for the sake of a righteous remnant, to provide another season for repentance and spiritual renewal. But does a Christian remnant really stand in the gap today, agonizing over the nation's sins, pleading with God to delay punishment for one more possible turning-time in the life of the people? (CH)

During the past twenty-five years American evangelicals have in fact several times failed to walk through open doors that might spectacularly have set their cause ahead with important consequences for the nation's religious fortunes. (COT, 383)

There is a coalescence of two forces right now. On the one hand there is an accelerated decline of American culture morally and spiritually. On the other hand there is a dynamic upsurge of the evangelical movement with its demonstrated life-transforming dynamic. These two trends happen just now to coincide and nobody can quite tell what the coalescence of those two trends will signify. (VP)

Christians can still make a difference in a world moving toward the End of All Ends and in a fast-declining nation not yet past redemption's point. The good news that God's grace can save us, can unleash a fresh tide of moral power and spiritual renewal, should be heralded from housetops, trumpeted on television, relayed on radio. (WS)

Nothing is more needed than national repentance on the part of people ungrateful for their blessings, and unwilling to make the moral sacrifices requisite for national well-being.

The times cry out for spiritual renewal alive to the high claims of divine truth and universal morality, for ethical dedication to neighborly good will, to human rights and duties under God. A nation that settles its political specifics in this context cannot go far wrong, and even when it does, it has a built-in method of correcting its mistakes. (CT)

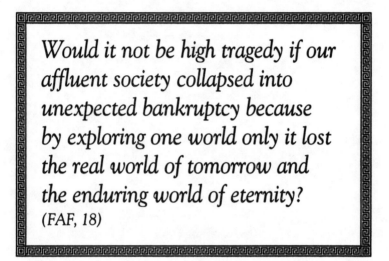

Would it not be high tragedy if our affluent society collapsed into unexpected bankruptcy because by exploring one world only it lost the real world of tomorrow and the enduring world of eternity?
(FAF, 18)

AUTHORITY

The problem of authority is one of the most deeply distress-ing concerns of contemporary civilization. Anyone who thinks that this problem specially or exclusively embarrasses Bible believers has not listened to the wild winds of defiance now sweeping over much of modern life. Respect for authority is being challenged on almost every front and in almost every form. (GRA IV, 7)

The problem of authority, which haunts all arenas of thought and life today, turns ultimately on the reality of God in his revelation. (WS2)

The chief problem of mid-century thought is the problem of authority. The problem is posed by a multiple inheritance: the Hebrew-Christian tradition, with its uncompromising claim to special revelation; the Graeco-Roman classic philosophy and modern idealism, with their case for the supernatural divorced from the miraculous; ancient natural-ism, Renaissance and contemporary empiricism, and modern scientific positivism, with their reduction of man to complex animality and of all reality to nature. (PD, 214)

The problem of authority centers in the query, do we have an authoritative revelation of God and, if so, is it rightly con-ceived as a word of God in the traditional sense? If it is not rightly conceived in these terms, how could those to whom any actual revelation came have so misunderstood its inner content? If they were wrong about the nature of revelation, can they be trusted as to the actuality of revelation? But is it as apparent as some modern religious philosophers would have us believe that they were wrong in their statement of the nature of revelation? (PD, 216-17)

For mankind today nothing is of greater importance than a right criterion whereby men may identify the truth and the good over against mere human assertion. (GRA IV, 16)

The Bible still stands provocatively at the heart of the human dispute over truth and values, over the nature of the real world, and over the meaning and worth of human survival. (GRA IV, 22)

The Risen Lord declared that 'all authority' had been given to him; nobody therefore has license to exercise authority as an independent prerogative unanswerable to him. (CH)

BIBLE

That God has been pleased to reveal his will, that he has done so in express commands, given to chosen men through the medium of human language, and available to us as the Word of God in written form, is so clearly the historic conviction of the Hebrew-Christian movement as to be virtually an indisputable characteristic. (CPE, 264-65)

The Christian faces the world armed with a truly creative word, a word that is intelligible, authoritative and enduring. What originally gave and still gives power to the Word of God is not tradition somehow brought to life by it, or architecture and ritual that some trust to impart potency to proclamation. Nor is sincerity by the one who proclaims the Word the key to its power; many human beings after all have been sincerely wrong. What lends power to the Word is rather that God himself is pledged to be its invisible and invincible herald; he tolerates no fruitless proclamation of his Word; he has ordained fulfillment of its mandated mission. (GRA IV, 493)

Everywhere around us is strewn the philosophical wreckage of those who rely only on the voice of conscience, on social utility, on aesthetic gratification, on majority consensus—on everything but a sure Word of God. (TGC, 44)

Amid the sensational enthusiasms of both secular and religious thought the Bible remains our best guide to prophetic sanity. (GRA IV, 497)

27

Apart from the Bible no firm reply exists against the rampant unbelief and strident skepticism of our age, no sure way around the contorted detours of modern culture, no lasting alternative to the extraordinary evils that plague our generation. (CMSS, 34)

The moral fortunes of the West hinge both in the past and in the present upon the fate of the Bible and on appropriation or neglect of its spiritual and ethical realities. (CCDC, 28)

Neglect of the main elements of biblical revelation renders most modern intellectual centers powerless. (CT)

The Bible is still the most incisive critic of our age. It confronts our broken love of God, our dull sense of justice, our shameful moral nakedness, our waning sense of ethical duty, our badly numbed consciences, our clutching anxieties, the ghastly horrors and brutal violence of this era. (WT)

The biblical prophets are far from outmoded; they are far ahead of us. They provide landmarks that we need more than ever in the dense forests of subjectivism to which modern speculation abandons us. (WT)

Inerrancy

The first thing the Bible says about itself is not its inerrancy or its inspiration, but its authority. . . . Just as in the Gospels the most important thing is the incarnation, death and resurrection, while the how of the incarnation, the virgin birth, lies in the hinterland; so also in respect to the doctrine of Scripture, while inspiration is as clearly taught as the virgin birth, it lies rather in the hinterland. The Bible teaches its authority and inspiration explicitly, while inerrancy, it seems to me, is an inference from this. (TS)

It is no accident that those who deplore the concept of biblical inerrancy are increasingly uncomfortable with the doctrine of biblical inspiration as well, and prefer to speak instead, sometimes quite amorphously at that, only of the authority of Scripture. (GRA IV, 194)

Those who reject inerrancy have never adduced any objective principle, either biblical, philosophical, or theological, that enables them to distinguish between those elements which are supposedly errant in Scripture and those which are not. (TS)

The familiar rejoinder that no one can exhibit the errorless autographs need not discomfit evangelicals in their claims about the inerrant originals. The critics similarly can furnish none of the errant originals that they so eagerly postulate. . . . The supposed errant originals are as hard to come by, if not more so, than the inerrant originals. (GRA IV, 208)

Inerrancy is the evangelical heritage, the historic commitment of the Christian church. (GRA IV, 367)

An unregenerate inerrantist is spiritually worse off than a regenerate errantist. But an unstable view of religious knowledge and authority jeopardizes not only an adequate definition of regeneration but one's insistence on its absolute necessity. The alternatives therefore seem much like choosing whether to have one's right or left leg amputated. (E)

Biblical Criticism

If one asks what, in a word, eclipsed the biblical doctrine of the inspiration of Scripture, what stimulated theological redefinition of inspiration in nonconceptual categories, and what encouraged neo-Protestant denial of inspiration as a decisive New Testament concept, the answer is modern biblical criticism. (GRA IV, 75-76)

The Bible has destroyed more critical theories and humbled more critics than they would have you believe. (WS)

Critics have been wrong in insisting that the Hittites were fictional, that there was no writing in Mosaic times, that most biblical Psalms date to the Maccabaean period, that supposed scriptural descriptions of the glories of Solomon's kingdom were exaggerated. They have been wrong in dating the biblical wisdom-literature in exilic or post-exilic times, claiming that worship of Yahweh originated with seventh-century prophets, that the Hebrew exile was a product of imagination, and so on. (GRA IV, 353)

Even liberal thinkers now warn modern biblical scholars that their critical partitioning of the Bible has led to irreconcilable disagreements, and that the time is long overdue to hear the biblical canon in its comprehensive unity. (COT, 389)

Old and New Testaments

That the one eternal and sovereign God created the world and all things by divine fiat; that man was created in the divine image, and hence possessed a distinctive dignity, being made for personal fellowship with Deity; that man, by voluntary revolt, fell from original righteousness into a state of moral and spiritual revolt; that salvation is impossible of attainment by human effort but is a provision of the God of holy love, who through His prophets promised a vicarious mediation from the divine side; that the provision of salvation is to be realized within history itself by the God who in a special way reveals Himself to His chosen people—what are these, but affirmations which stand at the core of the Old Testament, no less than of biblical Christianity? (DWT, 25)

The Old Testament necessarily awaits its own supersession; it bears latent within, the pledge of its future development and consummation. Christianity, if not wholly new, was not shrinkable to the Hebraic revelation; such a view would cancel out entirely the phenomenon of the entrance of Jesus Christ into history. From the New Testament perspective,

Judaism lacks its climax, and halts short of its proper terminus and crown. (DWT, 26)

The Christian church has insisted from the outset on the essential unity of Old and New Testaments, emphasizing that the Old Testament bears an indispensable testimony to Jesus Christ, and that the New Testament—albeit in terms of fulfillment—expounds no salvation other than that which is implicit and explicit in the Old Testament. (GRA III, 101)

Over and above particular prophecies, the New Testament sees in Jesus Christ the climax and comprehensive fulfillment of the entire Old Testament. It is not simply in a few scattered texts that the ancient witness to Christ is to be discovered; the Old Testament in its entirety testifies to the truth that salvation is not an attainment of sinful human effort but is a divine provision from above, a merciful gift and work of God, centered in the promised Messiah who is at once prophet, priest and king. (GRA III, 135)

While the New Testament doctrine of God is deeply rooted in Old Testament revelation, it also stands in significant respects on its own independent ground in view of the supremacy of the revelation in Jesus Christ, the fuller gift of the Spirit, and the role of the inspired apostolic teaching. (GRA V, 19)

Proposals to treat the Gospels as historical novels inexcusably superimpose a modern literary form on first-century literature. (GRA IV, 351)

The New Testament sets forth a number of basic Christian principles. . . . It does not endeavor to specify rules for the whole of life. If there are principles, as undoubtedly there are, these should assuredly be applicable to particular cases. These are to guide the Christian in the choices he makes. He must see himself, his motives, and his desires clearly. He must know the New Testament principles for conduct, which apply here, which do not, and why. Then he must decide and act. Thus, by this terrifying and responsible process, he matures ethically. There is no other way. (CPE, 419)

No book has been translated into as many languages and versions as has the Bible. As the inspired Word of God, it still shows itself strong and irresistible even behind the iron curtains of geopolitical conflict and the velvet curtains of ecclesiastical neglect. (GRA IV, 161)

The Bible remains God's hot line to this generation. (NSF, 11)

The world dreads to open its morning newspaper; does the church still rejoice to open the Bible? (NSF, 100)

CHRISTIANITY

Feuerbach and Marx both thought that by our time Christianity would lie buried with the Homeric myths, and some exuberant naturalists have claimed that scientific knowledge explains God away. Christianity has meanwhile become the first religion to gain a world presence, and even in some Asian and African countries it has become the fastest growing force. Where communism tries to extirpate it or to drive it underground, it becomes purified and deepens its commitments. In Latin America those who profess it anew are largely the working class. (WT)

From the very first, Christianity appealed to the intellect. Revelational theism has never offered itself as an escape from rationality; rather, it has insisted on the subrationality or irrationality of all other views of reality. (RMM, 219)

Faith is no less an integral factor in scientific thought than in religious thought; indeed, faith is an element in all human understanding. Faith supplies the canopy idea that identifies, explains and evaluates data in which scientists or historians or theologians are interested. What distinguishes blind faith from genuine faith is the presence of verificational supports—non-empirical or empirical—and the logical power or consistency attending explanatory principles. Biblical faith finds its verificational supports in the revealed Word of God; it claims that God in his revelation more comprehensively and consistently explains the data of being and life than any other alternative. (WS3)

33

A religion claiming absolute revelation, and hence an authority universal in time and space, must explain the past, no less than the present and future. Christianity came into the world as the fulfillment of all genuine religious desire, but especially as the completion of the Hebrew claim to special revelation. (DWT, 24-25)

To say that Christianity is unique is not enough—every religion has distinctives. (PED, 76)

Christianity explains the universality of religion by the fact that God is real and has revealed Himself; the multiformity of religion it explains by man's sinfulness. For it, the plurality of religions is not an evolutionary development from some common religious essence; rather, the diversity of religions is due to a sinful devolution, through demonic influences, of God's universal revelation of himself. (NSF, 43)

Christianity is a faith—but so are Buddhism, shamanism, communism and humanism. The main issue for the intellectual world is whether the biblical revelation is credible; that is, are there good reasons for believing it? I am against the paradox mongers and those who emphasize only personal volition and decision. They tell us we are to believe even in the absence of good reasons for believing. Some even argue that to seek to give reasons for the faith within us is a sign of lack of trust or an exercise in self-justification. Against any view that faith is merely a leap into the dark, I insist on the reasonableness of Christian faith and on the "rationality" of the living, self-revealed God. I maintain that God creates and preserves the universe through the agency of the Logos, that man by creation bears the moral and rational (as opposed to irrational) image of his Maker, that despite the Fall, man is still responsible for knowing God. I believe that divine revelation is rational, that the inspired biblical canon is a consistent and coherent whole, that genuine faith seeks understanding, and that the Holy Spirit uses truth as a means of persuasion, that logical consistency is a test of truth, and that saving trust in Christ necessarily involves acceptance of certain revealed propositions about him. (CT)

The phrases "modern culture," the "scientific era," and their like, are not empty catchwords; they stand for an inner spirit which has forced Christianity to fight for its very life. . . . The central calendrical reference was now to become not the Christian divide, but, in the spirit of Copernicus and Darwin, the vast antiquity in the hidden recesses of the evolutionary process. (DWT, 36)

Christianity knows—and it dare not forget nor let the world forget—that what the social order most needs is a new race of men—men equipped not simply with new textbooks and new laws, but with new hearts. (ACSE, 30)

Part of our problem today is that people put on Christianity like a pair of Totes in rainy weather. (WT2)

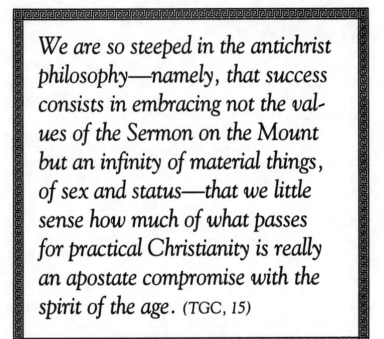

We are so steeped in the antichrist philosophy—namely, that success consists in embracing not the values of the Sermon on the Mount but an infinity of material things, of sex and status—that we little sense how much of what passes for practical Christianity is really an apostate compromise with the spirit of the age. (TGC, 15)

CHURCH

The church is not primarily a building that posts hours of public access; it is an assembly or fellowship of believers. (TGC, 87)

Christ founded neither a party of revolutionaries, nor a movement of reformers, nor a remnant of revaluators. He "called out a people." The twice-born fellowship of his redeemed Church, in vital company with its Lord, alone mirrored the realities of the new social order. This new order was no mere distant dream, waiting for the proletariat to triumph, or the evolutionary process to reach its pinnacle, or truth to win its circuitous way throughout the world. In a promissory way the new order had come *already* in Jesus Christ and in the regenerate fellowship of his Church. (ACSE, 28)

Though the church of Christ will always be a minority "called out of the world," it is ideally a minority that holds an ideological initiative in the battle for men's minds and wills and consciences. It is ideally a minority that cannot be ignored, a minority that shatters the complacency of its self-confident contemporaries, a minority that sounds an eerie warning and voices an authentic hope to an uneasy and unstable generation. (FAF, 177-78)

To a rebellious race, in which she recognizes her own immediate and renegade past, the church witnesses of her own grateful reception and appropriation of the given revelation of God. . . . As a new society that functions by the ideals

37

and dynamics of a freshly appropriated way of life, the church brings the hesitant world around her under the purging fire of the age to come, and bears expectant witness to the coming King. (GRA II, 16)

The Christian religion connects the prophetic vision of the messianic community or new society with the New Testament church as a global, transnational fellowship that embraces regenerate Gentiles and Jews alike. (GRA III, 121)

The new society is a society that is transracial, transcultural, transnational, and in which love ideally reigns in all interpersonal relationships. (S)

The church of Jesus Christ is a community, not a clique. (NSF, 51)

It is impossible for believers to opt out of the body of Christ. We need one another for well-being and survival, not simply for amusement and diversion. A body without some of its vital members is in need of radical surgery. (NSF, 51)

Every appeal to an inerrant Bible should humiliate us before the inerrant Christ's insistence on the unity of his church. (CMSS, 32)

It is one thing for denominations to reshuffle ecclesiastical furniture; it is another for believers worldwide to manifest their unity in Christ. (NSF, 54)

Ecumenism

The notion of an ecumenical age becomes mainly a public relations illusion. Major divisions in Christendom remain to be overcome, while the extent to which ecumenical merger has actually achieved Christian unity remains to be demonstrated. . . . Ecumenical mergers have substituted bigger denominations for smaller denominations. (GWSH, 128)

There is almost no enthusiasm going for ecumenism at the local level, and at the national level organized Christianity is in great confusion and retrenchment. (VP)

Both evangelical and nonevangelical crosswinds are currently too confusing to give a clear signal about any ecclesiastical realignment. (CT)

Ecumenism is an objectionable alternative rather than a glittering attraction, in the eyes of many evangelicals, because of evangelicalism's clear limits to doctrinal tolerances; ecumenical pluralism can and has embraced Unitarians, Swedenborgians, and even nontheists. (TGC, 82)

Although evangelicals have criticized the broad basis of ecumenical merger and unity, they have achieved in their own ranks few mergers on the theological-spiritual level they espouse. (ERCT, 82)

Today criticism of institutional Christianity is a flood at its crest, and the ecumenical movement now stands as a major specimen of institutional religion. Another massive religious institution is the last thing in the world a Muslim, Hindu, or Buddhist needs to be converted to. (NSF, 55)

Mainline Protestant denominations are under fire for funding revolutionary movements, compromising confessional theology, and yielding to parachurch groups the initiative for evangelical causes like student evangelism, scripture translation, orphan and child care, and pro-life concerns. (CMSS, 31)

Whenever the Church considers itself the conscience of the state, or the pulsebeat of the body politic, the damage it incurs by thus directly merging its interests with those of the world or the surrounding culture is no less serious than that inflicted on the political order by the Church's legislation of her patterns of behavior upon society in general. (ACSE, 113)

Never is the church more impotent than when she imposes on the world new standards that she herself neglects. (PED, 67)

The problems of modern ecumenism run fully as deep as its promise, and the Great Head of the Church alone can give full substance to its promise and give deliverance from its problems. The deepest need of the churches is not organizational merger but the gift of repentance, and their surest bonding element is in union with Christ and under him in devotion to his revealed truths and commandments. (GWSH, 138)

The Church's Responsibility

The prime need of the Church in these times is a new sense of its proper task. (ACSE, 10)

The church's primary duty in the public order is to enunciate the revealed will of God, to call man in society to the enthronement of it, and to exemplify in its own fellowship of love and righteousness the blessings of moral and spiritual obedience. (PED, 103)

The Church is not to blame for the world's predicament, even if she needs a much more profound strategy of Christian evangelism and Christian public involvement. (TGC, 35)

The church exists in fact not primarily in a mission to the world outside, but in obedience to the risen Head, and in his redemptive embrace. (FAF, 60)

Jesus Christ alone is Head of the church. He has no favored puppets, any more than he has a first lieutenant in Rome, and he assesses the Christian community with scrupulous honesty. He still walks among the churches, threatening to remove lamps from their candlesticks. (NSF, 52)

Destruction of the true church is excluded by Jesus Christ's resurrection, ascension, priestly ministry, and final return. He is the head of the body—the supernatural source of the church's distinctive life. (BPP)

Jesus Christ is head; not the Holy See, or an ecclesiastical magistracy, or a world ecumenical central committee. (CCDC, 90)

Even now, in the worst of times, the church is prone to resurrection. The Head of the body has already passed through death and resurrection and lives in the eternal order. Even now, he imparts powers and virtues that belong to the coming age, sharing with us a sample of our future inheritance. (BPP)

The question "Is it too late for the church?" cannot be answered by an abstract assessment of the contemporary religious scene. It is a question each of us answers by the measure of our love for Christ and for those who do not know Him. Do we consider it unworthy of mention to those at our side that Christ is risen from the dead, and that the Holy Spirit gives new life? Do we each day ask ourselves whether Jesus Christ truly reigns in us as Saviour and Lord, or whether we are hesitant disciples in bondage to the sin of silence? (NSF, 117)

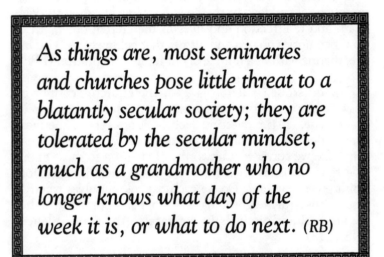

As things are, most seminaries and churches pose little threat to a blatantly secular society; they are tolerated by the secular mindset, much as a grandmother who no longer knows what day of the week it is, or what to do next. (RB)

CIVILIZATION

The savages are stirring again; you can hear them rumbling and rustling in the tempo of our times. (TGC, 15)

Flares of distress signals emblazon the whole field of human behavior. Christianity's millennium-long barricade against a resurging paganism is weakening before the onslaughts of iniquity. (CPE, 13)

A half-generation ago the pagans were still largely threatening at the gates of Western culture; now the barbarians are plunging into the oriental and occidental mainstream. As they seek to reverse the inherited intellectual and moral heritage of the Bible, the Christian world-life view and the secular world-life view engage as never before in rival conflict for the mind, the conscience, the will, the spirit, the very selfhood of contemporary man. (TGC, 27)

Both the pagan forces and the Christian forces have accelerated their initiative and seem increasingly locked into a life-and-death struggle. (TGC, 23)

Paganism is now more deeply entrenched than in the recent past, and it holds a firmer grip on Western society. Given the present historical dynamisms, my view is that in another half generation—before the turn of the century—humanism will have lost its humanism and the regenerate Church will survive in the social context of naked naturalism and raw paganism. (TGC, 23)

As in pre-Christian antiquity, a mood of melancholy—a questioning of the worth of personal survival—is falling once again over human history. (CCDC, 132)

Just as the sack and fall of Rome wrote a bloody picture finish to ancient civilization, so it is apparent that the plunder of Berlin and the atom-bombing of Hiroshima are gigantic visual aids disclosing the corruption and judgment of modern culture. (PD, 18)

These factors—the extensive loss of God through a commanding spread of atheism, the collapse of modern philosophical supports for human rights, the brutish dehumanization of life which beyond abortion and terrorism could encourage also a future acceptance even of nuclear war, and a striking shift of sexual behavior that welcomes not only divorce and infidelity but devious alternatives to monogamous marriage as well—attest that radical secularism grips the life of Western man more firmly than at any time since the pre-Christian pagan era. (TGC, 27)

The Twentieth Century

The most sudden and sweeping upheaval in beliefs and values has taken place in this century. No generation in the history of human thought has seen such swift and radical inversion of ideas and ideals as in our lifetime. (CMSS, 81)

We live amid the first effort in the long history of the West to erect human culture on godless foundations. (C)

The drift of twentieth-century learning can be succinctly summarized in one statement: Instead of recognizing Yahweh as the source and stipulator of truth and the good, contemporary thought reduces all reality to impersonal processes and events, and insists that man himself creatively imposes upon the cosmos and upon history the only values they will ever bear. This dethronement of God and enthronement of man as lord of the universe, this eclipse of the supernatural and exaggeration of the natural, has precipitated an intellectual and moral crisis that escorts Western civilization, despite its brilliant technological achievements, ever nearer to anguished collapse and atheistic suffocation. (CMSS, 84)

There is a very real danger that modern civilization will disintegrate and that we will be part of its debris. (WT)

All the struts of civilized society seem to be giving way today. The overarching question concerns the meaning and worth of human existence and survival; this embraces all the dilemmas of contemporary life, from the breakup of the family to abuse of drugs. (CT2)

A decisive verdict on civilization in our times and possibly an end-time judgment now hangs over the whole human race. (FAF, 47)

The intellectual decision most urgently facing humanity in our time is whether to acknowledge or disown Jesus Christ as the hope of the world and whether Christian values are to be the arbiter of human civilization in the present instead of only in the final judgment of men and nations. (WS)

Nothing can be clearer than that the medieval mind related to Christ, at least in intention, not only theology and worship, but also philosophy, government, art, music and literature. (DWT, 33)

Many scholars who claim to be emotionally detached and to view human events reflectively today voice direful predictions of impending doom, but mostly for the wrong reasons—overpopulation, famine, depletion of energy, ecological pollution, nuclear destruction, perhaps even asteroidal collision. These are not the worst of our woes, but they are trouble aplenty. . . . Even if we find a way around the pressing problems they indicate, the deeper facets of the civilizational crisis remain: the crisis of conscience, the crisis of truth, the crisis of will, the crisis of spirit—in short, the moral and spiritual dilemma that has overtaken our generation; the breakdown of authority; the confusion concerning transcendent reality; the subjectivizing of God; and with all this the loss of the worth and meaning of personal survival. (WS2)

Can Western civilization escape inner chaos and self-destruction if it faces the future without a significant role for transcendent justice and the revealed will of God? If you think not—as I think not—then your Christian commitment imposes upon you a heavy duty to share in the present effort to preserve the American republic and to warn and instruct all the modern powers that are marching off the map to join once-great nations of antiquity in their oblivion. (FAF, 118)

Culture

Hebrew-Christian thought, historically, has stood as a closely knit world and life view. Metaphysics and ethics went everywhere together, in Biblical intent. The great doctrines implied a divinely related social order with intimations for all humanity. The ideal Hebrew or Christian society throbbed with challenge to the predominant culture of its generation, condemning with redemptive might the tolerated social evils, for the redemptive message was to light the world and salt the earth. No insistence on a doctrinal framework alone was sufficient; always this was coupled with the most vigorous assault against evils, so that the globe stood anticipatively at the judgment seat of Christ. . . . The emperors must come to terms with Jesus, if not in this life then in the next. (UCMF, 38)

Never has the need for a culture enlivened by the moral law of God been more urgent than in our generation when social tumult obscures the very patterns of normalcy, and in fact increasingly champions the normless. In a culture dominated by a neo-pagan mind and will, deviation tends to become the norm, and normalcy in turn is perversely declared deviant. That cultural condition is the midnight hour for an evangelical alternative that seeks to count for something significant before the collapse and ruination of the contemporary social scene. (TGC, 124)

Young people today know the personal feuding that can and does blemish some of our evangelical movements and churches, even if we promote them as anticipatory fragments of the millennium. Young people today smile at our ready holding of a Bible in one hand while we offer a pointed defense of the status quo when we ought to be addressing God's clarion call of renewal to all of modern culture. They find themselves forced to read the radicals for a searching critique of the spirit of the age, and they pass harsh judgments that hurt us to the quick. (FAF, 26)

In two senses the Church goes counterculture. First, she disputes not only the corrupt practices but also the alien beliefs about God and ultimate reality that inspire non-biblical perspectives on life and the world. Second, she challenges the notion that a good society and just state can in fact be permanently sustained by unregenerate human nature. Christian culture presupposes both the Christian world-life view and the dynamic vitalities of spiritual regeneration. (TGC, 117)

Christianity is above culture, not anti-culture nor pro-culture as such. (TGC, 118)

If Bible-believing Christians can ride against the secular stream by mass evangelistic crusades aimed to rescue otherwise doomed sinners, they can summon enough courage and concern in public—at least, I am convinced they can, and will, if fully aroused to the urgency of these times—to stand against the culture in majestic witness to the holy commandments of God. (PED, 7)

Successive cultures have their half-day, and except for the perpetuity lent them by anthropologists and historians, they fade, along with their gods, into oblivion. (GRA V, 9)

The mindset of modernity is but a transitory phenomenon. But it will exploit the illusion of permanence if we do not effectively exhibit its weaknesses and more importantly exhibit the superiority of the theistic view. Modernity is but an agonizing moment in the history of civilizations; only a view that has eternal validity can hope to be forever contemporary. (TGC, 142)

All the modern gods are sick and dying. The nations that long lusted after power are now terrified by it. Sex has played itself out for many who thought an infinity of it would be heaven on earth. The almighty dollar is falling like a burned-out star. It is a day made-to-order for sons of the prophets, for sons of the apostles, for Protestant Reformers, and for evangelical giants. (CCDC, 107)

The pagan option is always knocking at the door of the person who crowds God out of his or her life. (TGC, 59)

The barbarians are coming; the Lord Jesus Christ is coming. *Christians are here now; do they know whether they are coming or going?* (NSF, 133)

CREATION

The philosophical options concerning the origin of the universe reduce to three: either the universe has always existed, or it is self-caused, or it exists through an independent being who made it. (GRA VI, 124)

If the Christian doctrine of creation contains one central emphasis on *how* God created, it is that God created by the instrumentality of his Word and, moreover, that he created *ex nihilo*. (GRA VI, 120)

From its first moment of creation the space-time universe has been pervasively dependent on the Creator. Without his omnipresent power it would revert to the *nihil* of nothingness that prevailed before God's *ex nihilo* creation. (GRA VI, 455)

The idea of creation of the universe was unknown in ancient times except in Judeo-Christian revelation. In Jainism, one of the three major religions of India, the world has always been perceived as infinite and uncreated. And in Greek philosophy anything like a total creation or production of the material world was unknown. (GRA VI, 121)

Those who regard evolution as an intellectual fallout from the Christian view of origins, or as merely a speculative modern alternative to it, may be surprised that the theory reaches back to pre-Christian times. Evolution is a very ancient theory, one that has existed in many forms. (GRA VI, 156)

The striking contrast between biblical Christianity and other thought movements, whether religious or philosophic, will come to view immediately if, for the moment, we go behind the modern preoccupation with evolution. For, among the ancient traditions, it was the Hebrew-Christian movement alone which assigned an important role to time, without making time the ultimate explanation or ground of the universe, and without placing God in time. (NDG, 125)

To say that time is created is—as in the case of the whole creation, nature and man included—to say several things. It is not a non-entity, an unreality, an appearance merely; it has a derivative reality, and the word "reality" cannot be tampered with in the case of time any more than in the case of nature as a whole. In his relations with His creatures, God acts within the derivative reality of time; at "sundry times" he spoke to the fathers (Hebrews 1:1), and in "due time" he manifested his Word (Titus 1:3). Time is a created actuality; there is a beginning of time, an end-time and a "today" of spiritual salvation or rejection. (NDG, 132)

The origins of the earth and of the solar system are no nearer scientific explanation than is the origin of life. (GRA VI, 180)

The "rational" form that Darwin gave to earlier evolutionary speculation lay in his asserted scientific verification that all complex species arise slowly by chance variation and natural selection from simpler forms. (GRA VI, 157)

The creation-evolution conflict in public schools centers in the tendency of educators to present evolution as valid scientific truth, that is, as established dogma, and creation as myth. (GRA VI, 149)

The fact is that evolutionary humanism is a more rigid orthodoxy than is biblical religion: while professing to be empirically neutral it often views any who challenge its dogmas as heretics and tries to silence them as academic illiterates. (GRA VI, 151)

The big-bang theory, by assuming that the expansion or creation of the universe is a presently continuing phenomenon, aligns itself with theories of continuous creation that run counter to Scripture. . . . It also leaves unanswered the question of how the complex order and structure of the universe resulted from the immense explosion that it postulates. (GRA VI, 129)

Evolution

The big issue today is over gradual or spasmodic change, with the spasmodic clearly winning the field. Pro-Darwinian scholars project several theoretically possible harmonizations of gradual microevolution and episodic macroevolution. . . . But such explanations nonetheless compromise the Darwinian insistence on gradualism. (GRA VI, 165)

It·was actually scientists and not theologians who in the nineteenth century first encouraged the understanding of the created kinds or families of life in the narrow sense of species. When theologians then espoused this view they were challenged by scientists who had moved on to argue for the fluidity of species. (GRA VI, 109)

The subject of the mode of evolution is just as riddled with problems as that of the pace of evolution. (GRA VI, 166)

Evolutionary theories of human origin are embarrassed by the problem of Eve, since the appearance simultaneously of masculine and feminine forms of *Homo sapiens*, whether gradually or suddenly, would be unbelievably improbable on evolutionary terms. (GRA VI, 240)

The attack on entrenched evolutionary dogma is gaining a vehemence unprecedented since the turn of the century, with the noteworthy exception that today it is not theologians and clergy but rather scientists who are in its vanguard. (GRA VI, 162)

Biological evolution, a revisable theory that has already undergone much revision, is in some respects a useful theory even if it should be untrue. Gainful predictive premises have in fact not infrequently been a byproduct of theories that have later had to be abandoned. The assumption of man's emergence from an animal ancestry has led to medical experiments of immense benefit to humanity. To be sure, morphological and to some extent even psychic parallels could provide a basis for medical experimentation even if similarities were postulated on the basis of the divine creation of all creaturely life rather than of evolutionary development. (GRA VI, 177)

Christian theists can hardly be expected to harmonize the Genesis account with modern scientific theory at points of possible conflict unless they are told exactly what evolutionary premises its advocates consider beyond revision. (GRA VI, 196)

Since God is the creator of the space-time universe, any aspect of the created universe becomes idolatrous if taken to represent deity. Pagan worship of the sun, moon or stars, or of human or animal or other creaturely forms, creations which the Hebrews knew by revelation to be of divine origin, could be nothing other than worship of the creature in the Creator's stead. (GRA V, 217)

What is crucially at stake in the creation account is a distinctive world-life view. It openly repudiates the metaphysical and moral outlook of a world that worships the physical forces of the universe and in so doing loses the sovereign Creator of the world, and man as God's special image. (GRA VI, 118)

At the center of the entire Bible stands the living God. If we turn to Genesis 1 for information first and foremost about the cosmos and man we miss the center of its focus. The subject of Genesis is not quarks or quasars, but God. (GRA VI, 110)

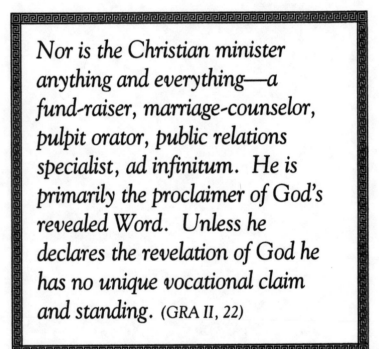

Nor is the Christian minister anything and everything—a fund-raiser, marriage-counselor, pulpit orator, public relations specialist, ad infinitum. He is primarily the proclaimer of God's revealed Word. Unless he declares the revelation of God he has no unique vocational claim and standing. (GRA II, 22)

EDUCATION

While popular education once recognized Christianity as its mother, yet the academic world has somehow come to treat supernatural religion as a disaffected mother-in-law and finally as an outlaw. (GWSH, 106)

We need to restore the educational system to a quest for the *whole* truth. (HP)

Just as pressures had mounted against the recognition of the reality of God in public education, so now they are mounting against any recognition of the reality of God in public life, and hence for separation of the state from God. (GWSH, 108)

Many public schools avoid the teaching of biblical theism as a sectarian prejudice while they accommodate the teaching of evolutionary humanism. (WS3)

My guess would be that on balance the secular universities more effectively communicate humanism than many of our religious colleges succeed in communicating biblical theism. (L)

Radical students more and more challenge the combination of raw naturalism with ethical imperatives. . . . The leftist students are saying to the professors, "We share your naturalism but we don't see how you get your ethics out of it." (HP)

For all the non-theistic orientation of most liberal learning, the most virile Christian witness has emerged from college and university youth who have found biblical vitalities outside their classroom studies and who now spiritually outpace many of their professors. (WS3)

While most students, even many who pursue studies in philosophy, delay any serious wrestling with metaphysical concerns, there are tens of thousands in the American evangelical movement whose personal faith in Christ and commitment to Christian theism dates back to high school and university. Their exposure to Judeo-Christian realities came not in connection with classroom studies but mainly on the margin of formal studies, through association with fellow students whose devotional vitality and moral dedication contrasted notably with the spiritual apathy and ethical permissiveness prevalent on the secular campus. (CMSS, 91)

When our Christian forefathers founded Harvard and Columbia, they did not have in mind merely salvaging the saints. (TGC, 96)

Two out of three of the colleges now existing in America were founded by the churches. (ERCT, 75)

Some traditionally religious colleges have swallowed humanist philosophy to the point of gastritis; mention significant works on theology and their students are tempted to reach for a sleeping pill. (CH)

Evangelical Education

Evangelical schools have channeled much notable leadership into modern society. Yet of some thirteen million American university and college students, less than ninety thousand are enrolled on campuses represented in the Christian College Coalition. Some of these campuses, moreover, too much take the secular institutions as a model, and critics ask whether concessions to alien views may not impair their effectiveness in conveying a cohesive Christian perspective. (TGC, 88)

It is crucially important that teachers and students recognize contemporary culture for what it is, grasp its controlling beliefs and behavior patterns, and do full justice to its intentions. Education taught in a cultural vacuum short-changes the student who must live his life, as we do, in a particular historical context and must understand its far-reaching implications. We are not contemporaries of Plato or of Paul or of Hegel but of Stephen J. Gould and Carl Sagan, who despise the supernatural and, even more, seem wholly ignorant of divine commandments and of revealed truths. (TGC, 92)

In an age when university learning has lost a cohesive center—in terms of an unchanging God and fixed moral values—evangelical campuses have the grand opportunity of exhibiting the comprehensive unity of truth and indispensable importance of mind, conscience, godliness and love. (RB)

The evangelical churches need more than ever to proclaim the revealed nature and purpose of the rational God of creation, the final reality of the Logos of God in contrast to the pretenses of "anti-Word reason," the liberating reason of the revealed Word of God, the redemptive power of the Logos become flesh. This requires a Christian ministry deeply devoted to the study and statement of the truth of God. It requires Christian colleges and seminaries dedicated not simply to overthrowing the secular empirical philosophy and its arbitrarily restrictive verifying principles, but dedicated equally to preparing a generation of evangelical scholars skilled in proclaiming the Christian way of knowing God and the means of verifying truth about the whole of reality. It demands nothing less than an exhibition in the context of the Christian knowledge of revelation and creation, of an authentic world-life view in which all the sciences, theology included, fulfill their legitimate role. (GRA I, 121)

Christian theism deserves better from its friends than from its foes. In contemporary society it is the evangelical community that often obscures the comprehensive and cohesive nature of the biblical view. Our colleges must recover the unifying character and explanatory power of revelatory theism. A sociology course that allows the *is* to determine the *ought*, a psychology course that merely sprinkles a few Scripture verses atop a secular theory of the self, a science course that views the creation account as poetic myth, soon amputates all the vital parts until the whole is ready for cremation. (TGC, 141)

The surge of enthusiasm for evangelism on many evangelical campuses and the existential mood of American life worked against a deep, stable, intellectual interest on the campuses. (E)

Evangelistic success more than the victory of truth has become the goal of some campuses. (TGC, 121)

Evangelicalism must develop a competent literature in every field of study, on every level from the grade school through the university, which adequately presents each subject with its implications from the Christian as well as non-Christian points of view. The bias and prejudice to which modern secularism yielded, in the very name of a revolt against dogmatism and in the supposed interest of impartiality, is becoming increasingly obvious to anyone familiar with the modern mood. Evangelicalism must contend for a fair hearing for the Christian mind, among other minds, in secular education. Almost every philosophic viewpoint can be taught by men who hold those convictions—whether Platonism, Aristotelianism, Kantianism, Hegelianism, or whatever else—except that the universities seem studiously to avoid the competent presentation of the Hebrew-Christian view by those who hold it. (UCMF, 70)

Higher Education

The evangelical colleges would do well to look anew at their curriculums and ask how best to enhance the excitement of serious learning in the present cultural context. Some are tempted to inject an activist dimension by involving students in social and political enterprises for academic credit. Some courses no doubt benefit from practical requirements. . . . But when such activism competes with time for serious study, and when the excitement of learning is shifted from the classroom to external activities, we need to remind ourselves that the world of ideas is the primary focus of an institution of learning that presumably functions as the intellectually critical center of culture. Without clear understanding of the Christian world-life view and a cohesive philosophy, evangelical activism will through its diversity and conflict nullify its own social impact. Somewhere an evangelical college may rise to the challenge of our culture by enrolling incoming freshmen in a course on Plato's *Republic* and on the great motifs of the Bible, and by sending seniors into our decadent society with a lucid comprehension of the Christian world-life view. (TGC, 89)

The higher the academic vision, the less evangelical monetary enthusiasm there is. (E2)

When the colleges emphasize not the intellectual fruits of their effort, but their evangelistic vitality or contribution, in order to encourage constituency support, they merely hide their failure to fulfill their distinctive mission. (RB)

I do not think that the focus of a liberal arts college should be reoriented toward student activism and campus politicization, nor do I think that the emphasis on metaphysical system and logical consistency are Greco-Roman liabilities rather than Judeo-Christian strengths. (COT, 76)

Christian education that is not intellectually demanding may be living on borrowed time. (TGC, 97)

My heart aches at times that the seminaries do not really know the time of the day, that it is virtually midnight for America and perhaps for the world. So often young people come with hearts aflame to learn how most effectively to bear witness to the world in our time and in a few short years they are defused of this passion. The percentage who do not finish their course, or who become vocational dropouts, seems of little concern to their mentors. (RB)

The seminaries are too often infused by worldly ambitions—size, endowment, electronic gadgetry, public relations. They too seldom recognize that just one Solzhenitsyn who speaks the truth boldly and is ready to suffer the consequences may put them permanently on the map in terms of their real mission. (RB)

Never have there been so many wasted young minds and rootless intellects. (CMSS, 60)

This is a time of cultural confusion. If the Christian point of view is going to be presented relevantly, by whom will it be presented, if not by alumni of schools specializing in Christian thought? (WR)

If evangelicals lose the battle for the mind of contemporary man it will be in their own colleges. (RB)

Christianity cannot long thrive in an atmosphere in which mass education is allowed to repress and impugn Christian confidence and conviction. (ERCT, 75)

EVANGELICALS

Evangelicals are to be known in the world as the bearers of good news in message and life—the good news that God offers new life on the ground of Christ's death and resurrection in the context of a biblically controlled message. (S)

Evangelical scholars are fully aware that the doctrine of the Bible controls all other doctrines of the Christian faith. (FMT, 138)

Evangelicals insist that although the Bible was written in particular historical and cultural milieus, it speaks with binding authority to our different historical and cultural situations. (CT)

Fundamentalism was a Bible-believing Christianity which regarded the supernatural as part of the essence of the biblical view; the miraculous was not to be viewed, as in liberalism, as an incidental and superfluous accretion. It was from its affirmation of the historic evangelical doctrinal fundamentals that modern orthodoxy received its name, and not from its growing silence on pressing global problems. (UCMF, 19)

Evangelicals do not dispute the fact that for a time at least Christianity may function with an impaired doctrine of Scripture. But it does so at its own peril and inevitably must then lose much of its essential message. (FMT, 139)

It is to the credit of evangelical Christianity that it has never defined its primary responsibility to be the unfruitful task of reorganizing unregenerate society. (ERCT, 65)

The whole range of biblical authority and authenticity was lost in the Social Gospel distortion of Christianity. Forfeited as well were the singular holiness of God, the awesome finality of divine command, the darkness and depth of human rebellion, the wonder of supernatural grace, the dependence of the church on Christ's resurrection life, and the Risen Lord's special commission to the church. (PED, 118)

The term "evangelical" is becoming a banner over many aberrations, and it increasingly means different things to different people. Some revel in "the day of the evangelical" and, to show how multitudinous the army is, boast of all possible varieties. Others define the term too narrowly and propose a purge list of "false evangelicals," thus pitting brother against brother in the body of Christ. (CT)

This character of fundamentalism as a temperament, and not primarily fundamentalism as a theology, brought the movement into contemporary discredit. Doubtless it is unfair to impute this mood of rancor and negation to the entire fundamentalist movement. Historically, fundamentalism was a theological position; only gradually did the movement come to signify a mood and disposition as well. Its early leadership reflected balance and ballast, and less of bombast and battle. (ERCT, 44)

If the strength of American evangelicalism rests in its high view of Scripture, its weakness lies in a tendency to neglect the frontiers of formative discussion in contemporary theology. (FMT, 140)

The evangelical phenomenon in the United States is broadening but not significantly deepening. (COT, 387)

Evangelicals tend to speak mostly to evangelicals rather than to the larger world. (CT2)

There can be little doubt of a resurgence of evangelical theology. All estimations of this renewal as merely an "undertow," or a marginal backlash of sorts, fail to do justice to its creative initiative and forward movement. (FMT, 125)

The day has now come for evangelicalism to rethink its whole building program. By tremendous outlay of funds, most church communities provide a worship structure which usually stands idle except for two Sunday services and a midweek prayer meeting, if the latter. No secular steward could long be happy about such a minimal use of facilities representing so disproportionate an investment. Out of the modern crisis may come a better stewardship. Perhaps the answer is the building of evangelical educational plants. . . . The time is here for an all-out evangelical education movement. . . . The maintenance of evangelical grade and high schools, and of evangelical colleges and universities, with the highest academic standards, promises most quickly to concentrate the thinking of youth upon the Christian world-life view as the only adequate spiritual ground for a surviving culture. (UCMF, 72)

The magnificent penetration that Billy Graham got at midcentury into the mainline denominations helped rescue evangelicals from their "fundamentalist ghetto" image. (E2)

Evangelicals can reinforce the scanty belief-structure of mainline churches, can import biblical missionary vitalities to reverse a declining membership, and can challenge bureaucratic manager-types interested only in sociopolitical change and who are disdainful of evangelicals as unsophisticated adversaries. (TGC, 77)

Twenty-five years ago there were signs that the long-caged lion would break its chains and roar upon the American scene with unsuspected power. The evangelical movement's mounting vitality baffled a secular press, beguiled by ecumenical spokesmen for liberal pluralism into regarding conservative Christianity as a fossil-cult destined to early extinction. . . . Having burst his cage in a time of theological default, the lion of evangelicalism now seems unsure which road to take. (ESI, 19, 24)

It is time that the evangelical movement sees itself for what it is: a lion on the loose that no one today seriously fears. (ESI, 96)

We may need for a season to be encaged in the Lion's den until we recover an apostolic awe of the Risen Christ, the invincible Head of a dependent body sustained by his supernatural power. Apart from life in and by the Spirit we are all pseudo-evangelicals. (COT, 392)

The . . . evangelical movement has too much tamed its fear of God; it sometimes performs as if it had the Lion of the tribe of Judah by the tail, and as if Christ were serving us rather than our serving him. (C)

Notwithstanding the evidence of ongoing vitality, the evangelical movement shows disturbing signs of dissipating its energies and of forfeiting its initiative. . . . Evangelicalism has shown itself painfully weak in shaping American national conscience. (ESI, 41-42)

What went wrong with "the year of the evangelical"? What skewed those presumptuous prophecies of evangelical awakening in America? (CCDC, 123)

It may well be that American evangelical leaders who basked in the limelight of news magazines and press coverage of their political influence and moral initiatives in national life will soon be stunned as the movement becomes a wilderness cult with no more public significance in a secular society than the ancient Essenes in the Dead Sea Caves. If so, however, it will not be simply because secular society has forced that fate upon us. It will be also because evangelicals have invited it by their shortsighted opportunism and their lack of a coordinated impact whose deepest resources are spiritual and ethical. (BPP)

For better or worse, diversification has increasingly become the hallmark of evangelicalism. (TGC, 73)

Can evangelicals square their multitudinous diversities with their profession of the inerrant authority of Scripture, a dilemma all the more problematic when biblical authority itself has become engulfed by dispute? Are the grounds of evangelical unity too dependent on "disavowals," too affirmatively slim, too lacking in doctrinal depth, to protect evangelicals from larger agreement with ecumenical agencies that view the ecumenical complex itself as God's ecclesiastical action, where church tradition often serves as a guide, and where a powerful hierarchy coexists with the affirmation of the universal priesthood of believers? (TGC, 80)

The disturbing fact is that no bold, creative counterproposal and counterassault exist to invade the educational, media and political arenas with a comprehensive alternative. No evangelical college, organization or publication presently charts that course. Contemporary evangelicalism lacks coordination of its theological, evangelistic and socio-cultural concerns. There is no broad evangelical vision, no commitment to dynamisms and goals sufficiently inclusive to contain and reverse the temper of the times. (COF, 397)

Unless evangelicals repair their multiplying frictions over social and political engagement in an intelligently spiritual meeting of mind and heart, the situation can only result in still further divisions that forfeit whatever impact might have issued otherwise through strategic cooperation. (ESI, 68)

What lies ahead for us—not a generation hence but right now—for an evangelical enterprise whose subsurface rivalries and breakaway movements continue to frustrate any overall comprehensive thrust? What awaits a movement if its idolized spokesmen are given more to polemics than to theological precision, more to public relations or to national image than to powerful convictions, more to team patriotism than to creative vision, more to statistics than to substance? (CCDC, 123)

By failing to transcend their isolation and independency, evangelical Christians have virtually forfeited a golden opportunity to shape the religious outlook of the twentieth century. (NSF, 52)

If evangelical Christians do not join heart to heart, will to will, and mind to mind across their multitudinous fences, and do not deepen their loyalties to the Risen Lord of the Church, they may well become—by the year 2000—a wilderness cult in a secular society with no more public significance than the ancient Essenes in their Dead Sea caves. (EBC, 111)

At present no single leader or agency holds the full enthusiasm and respect of every element within contemporary American evangelicalism. (ESI, 71)

Twenty-five years ago I had less awareness of how readily religious boards buckle under the influence of monied interests, more hope that institutional rivalries could be transcended, more belief in the selflessness of evangelical leaders, and much confidence that evangelical cooperation would forge a Christian world-life response to secular learning and cooperatively mount a powerful witness in public affairs. (BPP)

The evangelical community tends to reduce its task in society to negation rather than recognizing the need to construct a full-orbed Christian alternative. (CT2)

There is a growing awareness in Fundamentalist circles that, despite the orthodox insistence upon revelation and redemption, evangelical Christianity has become increasingly inarticulate about the social reference of the Gospel. The conviction mounts that the relationships of the church to world conditions must be reappraised, even if the doctrinal limits are regarded as fixed within which solution is likely to be found. . . . Fundamentalism is wondering just how it is that a world-changing message narrowed its scope to the changing of isolated individuals. (UCMF, 26)

The social reform movements do not have the active, let alone vigorous, cooperation of large segments of evangelical Christianity. . . . Such resistance would be far more intelligible to nonevangelicals were it accompanied by an equally forceful assault on social evils in a distinctly supernaturalistic framework. But, by and large, the Fundamentalist opposition to societal ills has been more vocal than actual. . . . The great majority of Fundamentalist clergymen, during the past generation of world disintegration, became increasingly less vocal about social evils. (UCMF, 17-18)

That Christian supernaturalism . . . should be accused of having lost its own devotion to human well-being is indeed a startling accusation. (UCMF, 20)

This modern mind-set, insisting that evangelical supernaturalism has inherent within it an ideological fault which precludes any vital social thrust, is one of the most disturbing dividing lines in contemporary thought. . . . It dismisses Fundamentalism with the thought that, in this expression of the Great Tradition, the humanitarianism has evaporated from Christianity. (UCMF, 23)

The flank of secular humanism cannot be turned without a penetrating social movement, and fundamentalism alone—as a network of independent stars—was more positioned to function as a political nuisance, or at best a moderating force, than to achieve a significant cultural breakthrough. (TGC, 75)

The coming decade of decision will be marked either by evangelical penetration of the world, or by the world's penetration of the evangelical movement and an inner circle's reactionary withdrawal into some modern Dead Sea caves. . . . The theological instability of some educational institutions and approaching retrenchment of evangelical colleges, the unending proliferation of evangelical independency, the decline of formative cultural impact, are eventualities which evangelicals must now accept in the absence of any comprehensively compelling alternative. (COT, 402)

The evangelical movement has problems enough of its own, but at least it was a movement, even if its cohesiveness was increasingly under strain. There is in fact much to hearten the evangelical mainstream: the continued visibility and impact of Billy Graham crusades; the multiplication and growth of conservative churches; the missionary umbrella of the Evangelical Foreign Missions Association and of the Independent Foreign Mission Association with a combined world outreach of eighteen thousand. (TGC, 76)

The American evangelical movement today, encamped between fundamentalism on the right and ecumenism on the left, appears more vulnerable to realignment than for a generation. (TGC, 73)

Unless another Great Awakening sweeps them, the evangelical churches may find themselves groveling on the sidelines of modern history. (NSF, 49)

The real test of an evangelical awakening is when public conscience judges itself by biblical criteria, even though it may not be personally committed. (SB)

Townspeople will recognize the living Lord's disciples once prayer meetings are again filled, once offenders repent and make restitution, once believers manifest a joy in living that escapes their world-steeped neighbors, once those neighbors are loved as "family." (TGC, 83)

The Christian Church—or some significant remnant of it—may indeed experience renewal, and it may even achieve spectacular gains on Mainland China and in certain African and Asian Third World countries. But that is another story, one marginal to the moral destiny of the West and to the fate of American evangelicalism. (TGC, 23)

Traditional evangelical hand-me-downs are inadequate for this turning-time in history. (CMSS, 18)

I have two main convictions about the near-term future of American Christianity. One is that American evangelicals presently face their biggest opportunity since the Protestant Reformation, if not since the apostolic age. The other is that Americans are forfeiting that opportunity stage by stage, despite the fact that evangelical outcomes in the twentieth century depend upon decisions currently in the making. (COT, 381)

Fifty years ago I had, as a young Christian, grand visions of the world impact of evangelical Christianity; today, as a time-worn believer, I still dream at times of the movement's profound potential. Admittedly, it is difficult, especially in the latter years, to distinguish dreams from hallucinations. (COT, 402)

God has not suspended the fate of the church in the world on American evangelicalism. It may well be that the evangelical church will rise to new spiritual power in unpredictable places and in ways that will avoid the weaknesses of contemporary American evangelicalism. A new and spiritually renewed evangelicalism may, in fact, arise in America—one that drives the present evangelical power-brokers to their knees. (BPP)

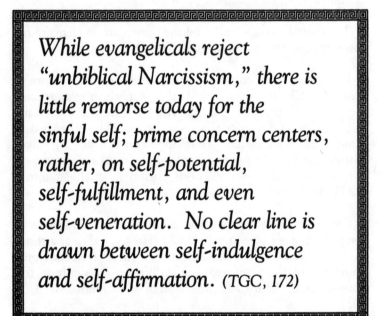

While evangelicals reject "unbiblical Narcissism," there is little remorse today for the sinful self; prime concern centers, rather, on self-potential, self-fulfillment, and even self-veneration. No clear line is drawn between self-indulgence and self-affirmation. (TGC, 172)

EVANGELISM

If the example of Jesus is any criterion at all for us, we ought not linger unduly in the pious isolation of the temple, but rather go out and speak out to the worst and best of unregenerate men concerning new life in Christ. (EBC, 51)

In the global crisis of our time—perhaps the consummating crisis of all time—if evangelical faith is to command attention, it needs courageous young men and young women as leaders. The cause of the gospel today needs disciples young enough to run to the tomb and to soar over the seas and to leap into space with good tidings. (NSF, 64)

The Church's primary duty is to expound the revealed Gospel and the divine principles of social duty, and to constrain individual Christians to fulfill their evangelistic and civic responsibilities. (ACSE, 10)

The New Testament meaning of the term *gospel* is clear and precise: the gospel is the good news of God's merciful rescue of an otherwise doomed humanity through the mediatorial life and work of Jesus Christ. (GRA III, 63)

A religion that speaks of forgiveness without a doctrine of substitutionary mediation and atonement has nothing in common with either Old Testament or New Testament religion. (GRA, 369)

One misses the whole meaning of the Gospel unless he realizes that, basic to all else, it is *good news*. The Greek verb for "evangelize" means literally to "address with good tidings." There is a timeliness about the Gospel for every man in every succeeding generation. (SCP, 26)

The Gospel resounds with good news for the needy and oppressed. It conveys assurance that injustice, repression, exploitation, discrimination and poverty are dated and doomed, that no one is forced to accept the crush of evil powers as finally determinative for his or her existence. (GRA IV, 542)

If evangelical Christianity offers a richness of life not for sale in the Secular City, if it heralds a hope that can warm the coldest heart, if it guarantees a future that can surpass the prospect of a sojourn on the moon, if it can open the modern soul once again to the transcendent world, if its revelation of God can demonstrate the power and joy of new life in the spirit, then now—*now*—is the time to trumpet the good news. (NSF, 24)

If hope is to prevail in our time, we who know God's transforming mercy and power must become roving tentmakers in the service of Christ who pitched his tent in a terribly wicked world and unveiled, for all to see, the glory of our life-renewing God. (CMSS, 150)

Every method of not evangelizing is wrong. Some methods [of evangelizing] surely are better than others, some more appropriate than others in different circumstances. Even from a timid gulp in an emotion-streaked testimony God can still get glory. (CMSS, 50)

The best method is, always has been, and always will be person-to-person evangelism. (CMSS, 51)

Evangelical deathstyle can in our generation be as important as evangelical lifestyle for the cause of evangelism. (CMSS, 60)

I don't think every seminary classroom should be turned into a course in evangelism but there's something wrong if divinity professors consider their courses so irrelevant to fulfillment of the Great Commission that nowhere in the span of a year's teaching do students get any glimpse of personal concern for the lost. (RB)

Nothing in the New Testament encourages the idea of world conversion. (TGC, 35)

Will it be said of us: They came to Berlin pondering their individual tasks in a world out of joint; they returned like a host from heaven, unable to stifle their praise of Christ, their thousand tongues swelling into a single mighty voice, and their lives glowing with the radiance of messengers from another world? (WCE)

To the world we seem like Hogan's army waiting for Godot. Can we take a holy initiative in history? Can we once more strike an apostolic stride? Can we put an ungodly world on the defensive again? Can we show men the folly of opposing him who has already overcome the world, of rejecting fellowship with the coming King? Will we offer civilization a realistic option, or only a warning of impending doom? Will Christianity speak only to man's fears and frustrations, or will it also fill the vacuum in his heart and crown his longings for life at its best? (NSF, 133)

Their risen Lord's "Go!" was the thrust that sent them to the ends of the earth. (PED, 64)

To men everywhere they witnessed of the crucified and risen One not simply because he commanded it—although Jesus did in fact dispatch them to the ends of the earth—but because the whole creation's future was implicit in His resurrection, was pledged and guaranteed by it, was in fact dependent on the direction and outcome of His conquest of sin and death. They invited men everywhere to partake of new life, to meet the coming King, to relate themselves to the coming kingdom of God. (FAF, 18)

Not until the Holy Spirit was poured out did Jesus release the church to witness. (NSF, 92)

Christians remind all mankind that the Christ who reigns tomorrow is not only Jesus of Nazareth who came yesterday, but is also the risen Lord of the church, who through this redeemed body of humanity signals the tidings that no one need permanently consign himself or herself to a living hell, whether here or hereafter. (GRA IV, 554)

Social Responsibility

Everyone must feel an obligation to the needy neighbor at his side. But Christians have a powerful motivation for doing so in their awareness that all mankind bears God's creation-image, and that Christ died for all. (CH)

The Church dare not be interested in social injustices merely as an occasion for evangelism. She has a standing responsibility to the province of social justice. That responsibility is first and foremost the vigorous declaration of the great principles of social order enunciated in the Scriptures. (ACSE, 121)

We need a missiological theology alert to all the frontiers of human tragedy, abreast of the competing worldviews and confused cultures of our age. Our theology must embrace not only our continent whose poverty is specially focused in material aggrandizement and sexual libertinism, but a larger world also that accommodates unmitigated famine and unrelieved destitution, that copes with Islamic terrorism and Koranic or Soviet expansionism. (TGC, 56)

To stand in one's own generation moved by a lively concern for the spiritual fate and eternal destiny of all men, to move among them with a sense of moral responsibility and mission, to engage in the common struggle for survival, to disclose the secret of life in one's own commitment, to mirror the content of justice, to demonstrate the lordship of Christ in worship and work and leisure, belong, as I see it, to the hard reality of being a Christian. (GWSH, 47)

The Christian task force is now deployed world wide and strategically positioned for its witness. It is familiar with the languages used by a billion pagans and has ready access in the space and media age to virtually all who need to hear the gospel. (BPP)

Key '73 was perhaps ahead of its time when it proposed that in every city and village evangelical believers, irrespective of denominational and ecumenical affiliation or nonaffiliation, stand in an arm-to-arm witness to the entire community of the joy of a personal relationship to the Redeemer and to the rewards of Bible study. That same cooperative effort could in time have fashioned also a common local protest against grievous community injustice and might have projected ethical alternatives. (CMSS, 53)

Some observers estimate that 70 percent of the U.S. population remains unchurched and insist we are not as much removed from European heathenism as evangelical promotion implies. (CCDC, 124)

The distinction between home and foreign missions is a generation outmoded; Christianity again faces the apostolic task of seeking to transform an environment that is quite unilaterally hostile. (UCMF, 71)

Has evangelical witness reached a monotonous plateau? Have we come out of the ghetto into the culture mainly to preen ourselves in an increasingly immoral age? Can the church somehow break out of entrapment in the media culture? Do local congregations any longer yearn to be renewed in spiritual and ethical priorities? Are we now faced by a loss of momentum and a costly fallaway, perhaps by the deadly final apostasy? Is America headed for a crumbling of her once-magnificent evangelical institutions and influences? Is the nation morally and spiritually doomed by the cultural crossfire? (CCDC, 125-26)

Rededication to positive and triumphant preaching is the evangelical pulpit's great need. The note of Christ's lordship over this dark century, of the victory of Christianity, has been obscured. (ERCT, 68)

A Christianity without a passion to turn the world upside down is not reflective of apostolic Christianity. (UCMF, 28)

Perhaps somebody here is looking for a bomb shelter in which to propagate the evangelical faith. If so, let me propose a change on your reading list: retire your Bible to the Smithsonian Institute and get a copy of the Dead Sea scrolls instead. The Essene caves are waiting for you. You won't have to worry about the world outside. You won't even have to worry about neo-evangelicals. You won't have to worry about anything. And in A.D. 4000 some roving archaeologists from Mars may discover in those Judean hills that, during the great crisis of the twentieth century, Saint Kilroy slept here. (GWSH, 50)

Let other men proclaim another god, another Christ, another spirit, another book or word—that is their privilege and their peril. But if once again the spiritual life of our world is to rise above the rubble of paganism into which it is now decaying, it will be only through the dynamic of revelation, regeneration, and redemption, through the sacred message which once brought hope. We have a task to do, a task of apostolic awesomeness; let us rise to the doing. The hour for rescue is distressingly late. (ERCT, 86)

FAMILY LIFE

One child lost to the faith usually becomes a family lost to the faith, and not many generations later a whole community of unbelief is set in motion because of some earlier neglect of parental duties. (ACSE, 11)

Parental responsibility for shaping the ideas and ideals of the oncoming generation has priority. The example of time spent in prayer, worship, Bible study and church participation, the reading of quality books and magazines, the nature of social life, the way the family makes crucial decisions, and not least of all open conversation and discussion of cardinal ethical and religious concerns define the character of home life. (TGC, 87)

The home is the best environment for teaching respect for law, as rooted ultimately in the divine order of things, and for creating a climate that lifts personal reverence for law above external compulsion. (ACSE, 11)

The sanctity of family life as a decisive biblical concern raises a whole cluster of logically related contemporary issues including adultery, divorce, prostitution, and the lax media handling of moral permissiveness and casual sex. (CMSS, 103)

The evangelical Christian's social concern is first directed toward the family as the basic unit of society. He finds a hollow ring in the social passion for "one world" that simultaneously lacks indignation over divorce, infidelity, and vagrancy in the home. Because liberalism fails to see society as a macrocosm of the family, it is bankrupt to build a new society. (GWSH, 67-68)

Another evidence of the deepening secular inroad is the shifting pattern of sexual behavior. This is manifest in the increasing rejection of monogamous marriage, the ready accommodation of divorce and its penetration into the church community and even into the marital commitment of the clergy, the legitimation of homosexuality and of lesbianism as alternative lifestyles. (TGC, 26)

The Hebrews, over against humanity in general, knew the self-disclosing God's fatherhood in distinctive relationship to the community of faith, a fatherhood that enveloped Israel in Yahweh's special providence. The New Testament reveals the paternity of God even more deeply and fully than does the Old Testament. Like Judaism, Christianity, too, affirms a universal divine fatherhood on the basis of creation and acknowledges the special fatherhood of the Creator-Redeemer God in the Old Testament community of faith. In addition Christianity publishes an unprecedented disclosure of divine paternity that awaited full manifestation through the incarnation of the eternal Son, a fatherhood that involves intimate individual relationship between God and his believing children through God's adoption of them as sons in Jesus Christ. (GRA VI, 323)

The world of religion knows no more remarkable turn in the history of ideas than this, that the fatherhood of God should have been dramatically unveiled by the one person whom the inspired writings and countless millions of believers declare to have been born of a virgin, that is, without human paternity. (GRA VI, 313)

GOD

The concept of God is determinative for all other concepts; it is the Archimedian lever with which one can fashion an entire world view. (RMM, 175)

God is not the Great Perhaps, the clueless shadow character in a Scotland Yard mystery. Far less is he a nameless spirit awaiting post-mortem examination in some theological morgue. He is a very particular and specific divinity, known from the beginning solely on the basis of his works and self-declaration as the one living God. (GRA II, 7)

Not even Americans with their skill in probing the surface of the moon have any special radar for penetrating the mysteries of God's being and ways. Apart from God's initiative, God's act, God's revelation, no confident basis exists for God-talk. (GRA II, 8)

The whole history of unbelief may be summarized as a "calling God names"—sometimes blasphemous, sometimes ridiculous, always somewhat derogatory—indeed, as a refusal to identify him by his true name. (GRA II, 167)

From secular philosophers and even so-called secular theologians one now often hears that God is an incomprehensible idea for contemporary man: moderns allegedly find the idea of God unthinkable and meaningless. Much of this portrayal misjudges the epistemic predicament of secular man and in fact involves a basic and needless compromise with radically secular views. . . . Biblical theology insists that even the most radical secularist in his thinking and doing reflects some elemental awareness of God's claim upon human life, and that every man—the secular humanist included—has enough vital knowledge of God to invite divine judgment upon his personal rebellion. (GRA V, 14)

Theologians are woefully at odds over the nature and reality of God, the ways of theological knowing and the role and meaning of verification. This variance permeates even the most elite theological circles, including the prestigious membership of the American Theological Society, for example. Would the American Medical Association receive into membership a surgeon who denies the existence of man or a physician who denies the fact of human sickness? Would a geological society welcome into membership a scholar who insists that the earth is unreal as insistently as God-is-dead theologians exclude the ontological reality of divine being? (GRA I, 171)

The theologian is imperiled as well as the theological enterprise if he thinks biblical theism depends for its credibility and power upon speculative discoveries peculiar to our century, or to any century this side of the apostolic age. (TGC, 53)

In the existential encounter the God who supposedly "shows" never intrudes into history long enough to leave a calling card. (GWSH, 4)

The Bible not only records the authorized names of God, but it frequently speaks in the singular of the name of God. . . . The divine Name serves as a medium of revelation of the first magnitude, and denotes the self-revealed God as he desires to be known by his creatures. (GRA II, 172-73)

The false religions only stammer God's true name. (GRA II, 171)

Contemporary man seems to have lost God's address. But that is not all. He is unsure how to pronounce God's name, and, at times, unsure even of that name, or whether, in fact, God is nameable. (GRA V, 9)

To be sure, highly important differences distinguished logical positivist from existentialist interest in religious concerns. The logical positivist outlook is essentially antifaith, whereas the existentialist intention is often profaith. For the latter, God is real only in the decision of faith; for the former, the logical positivist, God is a nonsense syllable devoid of all meaning; only in the "faith" of the unenlightened is God real. . . . Both approaches despoil any rational case for theism by unjustifiably erasing all valid cognitive knowledge of God. (GRA V, 22-23)

The Bible also rules out many theories of transcendence, among them, for example, that God is incomprehensible or unknowable; that God is beyond all possible relationships to man; that God is wholly remote from nature; that God is superpersonal; or that his being the "Other" wholly precludes any possibility for human beings to bear aspects of the divine image. (GRA VI, 39)

Man can indeed know the God of creation and created reality—not exhaustively, to be sure, but nonetheless truly. (GRA I, 160)

The substance of God is, in the primary sense, nothing other than God himself; the divine substance is not an essence distinguishable from divine personality or from the divine attributes but is the very living God. God is therefore substance as existent reality, as opposed to nonbeing or mere appearance and shadow. (GRA V, 11)

God *who is* is the ultimate Who's Who, God who introduces himself. He is the standing God before whom every knee shall bow. (GRA V, 10)

For the Bible as a whole God is the infinitely perfect Spirit who freely reigns as Lord and Light and Love, and to whom all men and things owe their origin and continuance, and whose Messiah-borne mercy shapes the sinner's only ground of enduring peace and joy. (GRA V, 19)

The God of Christian orthodoxy is timelessly eternal. (GRA V, 239)

The living God is the immutable God who can neither increase nor decrease; he is not subject to development or decline. (GRA V, 286)

Only God is holy in himself. (GRA VI, 324)

Righteousness and benevolence are equally ultimate in the unity of the divine nature. (ACSE, 146)

God's truth distinguishes him as true in himself, veracious in all his words and deeds, author of all truth in the creaturely world, and foreign to all falsehood and pretense. (GRA V, 334)

It is God who makes himself known in self-revelation, who authorizes us to speak of what neither the nonbiblical religions nor secular philosophy discerned, namely, that three eternal personal distinctions coexist in the one living Godhead. (GRA V, 213)

No fact more directly establishes the uniqueness of the Christian view of God than that of the Trinity. It is God seen as triune and yet one—the doctrine of Trinitarian theism—which by a single declaration sets off the Christian view of God from all others. (NDG, 114)

Some critics consider orthodox representations of the Trinity a mathematical monstrosity; the doctrine, they contend, is as fallacious in its claim for the three-in-one God as is

the formula 3 x = 1 x. But this description patently distorts
the doctrine. Christian theology affirms neither that three
gods are one God nor that three isolated persons are one
God. Rather, it affirms three eternal personal distinctions in
the one God, in short, 3 x in 1 y. Such a formulation is both
intelligible and noncontradictory. It is, moreover, far less
complex than most mathematical formulas that engage
modern-day scientists. (GRA V, 165)

The Bible is monotheistic from core to circumference.
From its beginnings Christianity is no less irreducibly
monotheistic than Judaism. It unwaveringly joins the Old
Testament in insisting that the living God reveals himself as
the one and only God. (GRA V, 169)

Sovereignty

The Bible itself thrusts upon us the theme of divine predes-
tination. Calvin considers it a defrauding of believers to
withhold from them what Scripture says about their predesti-
nation. (GRA VI, 76)

The notion that God's foreordination destroys human
choice is countered by the emphasis that God's foreordination actually makes possible whatever agency man has ever
had and now retains. Were it not for God's eternal decrees,
man would not even exist as a morally responsible creature.
(GRA VI, 84)

God is not bound by any necessity of nature to the universe,
to mankind, or even to the church. He is free to create if and
as he wills, free to provide or not to provide salvation for fallen
creatures, free to covenant or not to covenant with the
Hebrews or any other peoples or with no one at all. He is free
also, if he wills, to graft Gentiles into the plan of redemption,
to call out a penitent church for global witness concerning his
ready forgiveness in Christ, and even to consummate history
by final judgment on all men and nations. (GRA VI, 76)

While men think that God is under antecedent obligation to them, that there is that in man despite his shortcomings which makes him in some essential sense spiritually and morally necessary to God, there the notion of the divine electing love becomes unintelligible. But when God is viewed as holy, and man as a sinner doomed to death, then the electing love of God—while not ceasing to retain its element of mystery—becomes more intelligible. When the line of human expectation is cut, in view of the divine holiness, then the line of divine love is cast from the eternities into the realm of time and the God of holy love is seen in special revelation, in redemption, in incarnation, and in glory. (NDG, 111)

The fact that human liberty is divorced increasingly from supernatural accountability may well become our national undoing. Yet a forced religious commitment is of no value either to God or to man. (CMSS, 11)

Recovery of God's sovereignty would furnish our generation once again with the only reliable constant in international relations, namely, the will of the holy Lord. (GWSH, 10)

If one believes that God is the supreme Sovereign, one will not be deluded by myths about Hitler or Stalin or Mao or by emperors like the Roman caesars or the German Kaiser Wilhelm, who proclaimed, "Deutschland Uber Alles!" (TGC, 119)

If one believes that God fixes the boundaries of the nations, one will know that it is not military might alone that ultimately will decide the fortunes of the United States or Soviet Russia or mainland China and Hong Kong. (TGC, 120)

A major theological development of the twentieth century is the increasing avoidance by theologians and philosophers—except in Roman Catholic and evangelical Protestant circles—of the term "supernatural". . . . One would think that the supernatural is mostly a matter of spooks and goblins. Even anthropologists who use the term mainly in connection with the animistic spirits of primitive religion seem unaware that the ancient Hebrews rejected animism and polytheism as idolatrous superstition and proclaimed instead the one supernatural God. (GRA VI, 11-12)

In the Bible God is the supernatural, while all heavenly spirits, whether fallen or unfallen, belong to the created world. (GRA VI, 21)

In certain important respects the Hebrew monotheistic revelation strikingly differs from Greek philosophical monotheism, one crucial difference being the forefront Hebrew emphasis on worship of Yahweh over against the rather secondary and subordinate role that Greek philosophy assigns to worship. (GRA VI, 72)

In a world given to worshiping the sun, moon or stars, or to referring the fortunes and misfortunes of life to astral determinism or to cosmic forces, the Genesis writer dares to emphasize that God created the heavenly bodies and that Elohim and Elohim alone is worthy of worship. (GRA VI, 110)

There is a secular swath of our society whose mindset against supernatural commitments is hardening into an atheistic *willset*. (WT)

Theism

The real alternatives to the discard of biblical theism were now seen to be not a restatement of classic idealism in modern dress, in which some elements of Christianity were retained, some rejected, and most of them transformed, but rather a thorough naturalism in which every trace of

Christianity, insofar as possible, would be eliminated. The genuine option was not a non-Christian metaphysics blended with a sub-Christian ethics, but an inversion which went the entire distance. (DWT, 55)

The intellectual suppression of God in His revelation has precipitated the bankruptcy of a civilization that turned its back on heaven only to make its bed in hell. (TGC, 143)

Atheism forfeits the resources that sustain even the tattered remnants of morality because it strips right and wrong of their transcendent and objective authority. (TGC, 170)

Biblical theism supplied the cognitive supports of Western culture. It adduced a linear view of history; it affirmed the sacredness of human life; it focused man's responsible role as steward of the cosmos; it nurtured the development of modern science; it engendered the compassionate humanitarian movements that differentiated Western society; it shaped the vision of a climactic end-time triumph of the good and of mankind's decisive deliverance from injustice; it offered the practical impetus and a means as well of transforming human existence into a New Society that exudes moral and spiritual power. (TGC, 125-26)

The sacrifice of a personal and purposive Creator and Sustainer of the universe led to new cosmologies that left unsure man's substance and status in the cosmos. (TGC, 127)

Revelatory theists have long stressed that secular humanism's social agenda is merely a cut-flower phenomenon doomed to wither for lack of metaphysical roots, and that it cannot logically withstand the rapid deterioration of cultural norms. (TGC, 129)

The disavowal of theism invited the decline of both idealism and humanism to unqualified naturalism. Neither the projection of an altruistic society nor the projection of a revolutionary utopia can long outrun a purposeless cosmos and history. (TGC, 132)

For man and society the loss of Biblical theism means the loss also of genuine liberation and humanism. (TGC, 133)

The frayed remnant of anthropological transcendence that secularists affirm is but the death rattle of an expiring theism whose strangulation neo-paganism eagerly anticipates. Since its rupture with biblical revelation, secular Western philosophy has progressively stripped away Christianity's arms and legs and head and heart—namely, its transcendent Creator, its purposive universe, its goal in history, and its unique incarnation of the Logos in Jesus Christ. (TGC, 133)

Revealed religion has always known that when man denies supreme allegiance to the eternal living Lord he inevitably worships some contemporary counterfeit. (GRA V, 9)

The false gods are always destined to become gods that were, gilded idols of the past whose imagined existence has given way. (GRA V, 9-10)

Only the self-revealing God can lead us even now toward a future that preserves truth and love and justice unsullied; all other gods are either lame or walk backward. (GRA VI, 9)

The emphasis on God's wrath, and along with this on the need of divine propitiation as a condition of the forgiveness of sins, is common to both Old and New Testaments. The New Testament focuses on the propitiatory death of Christ as at once the supreme revelation of God's love and of his righteousness. . . . The Bible insists on an essential difference, a qualitative distinction, between the anger and vengeance of the polytheistic gods and the wrath of the living, holy, self-revealed God of creation, redemption and judgment. (GRA VI, 329)

The real heroes of our time are those who in a faithless age hold, live and share their faith in God. Genuine revolutionary courage belongs to those who remain true to God even if atheistic rulers force them underground or punish citizens simply for being Christians. The true immortals will be those who seek to apply the principles of the Bible concretely to the complicated realities of modern life, who preserve a devout and virtuous family life, who are faithful to the abiding values of yesterday, today and tomorrow. (CH)

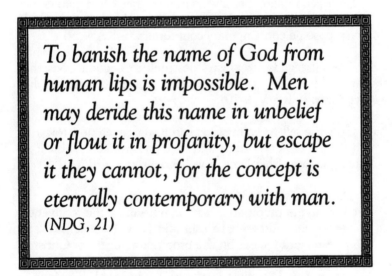

To banish the name of God from human lips is impossible. Men may deride this name in unbelief or flout it in profanity, but escape it they cannot, for the concept is eternally contemporary with man. (NDG, 21)

GOVERNMENT

Without the restraints of government to check men's evil lusts by the use of power in a sinful world, society would be reduced to anarchy. (PED, 32)

In view of the many modern totalitarian views that idolatrize the State as the lord of all life, the biblical exposition of the legitimate but limited authority of civil government gains special urgency. (ACSE, 84)

It is not the role of government to judge between rival systems of metaphysics and to legislate one among others. Rather government's role is to protect and preserve a free course for its constitutional guarantees. (CMSS, 80)

The Church has the right and duty to call upon rulers, even pagan rulers, to maintain order and justice. (ACSE, 81)

The Christian should be interested in government not only because it creates evangelistic opportunities but also because it preserves the social order and promotes justice as God's will for the fallen race. (ACSE, 95)

A moral imperative obliges civil government to punish crime and, more than that, obliges the state also to enforce capital punishment under highly limited conditions. (TGC, 69)

We stand in an interim period between Jesus' submission to the injustice of Pilate and his return as King of kings and

Lord of lords when every knee and all the rulers will bow—an interim period in which the New Testament ethic evolves with its legitimate role for the state as an instrument for active promotion of justice and restraint of injustice by the use of force. (S)

Civil government has in the purpose of God for history, this side of the end time, a role as a divinely structured order of preservation in fallen society as undeniable as his purpose for the church. (S)

Government cannot in any event be our salvation. The only real hope for security lies in a commitment to God's future. (WT)

Christians should promote respect for law without promoting an idolatry of law. They should be on the side of government and law and order as the ideal framework through which God seeks to promote earthly justice and peace in a fallen, pluralistic society. (L)

The great fault of contemporary civilization lies not in the public's disposition to overestimate the importance of law, but rather to underestimate it. (GRA VI, 435)

If evangelical Christians concentrate simply on moral and spiritual freedom to the exclusion of legal freedoms they not only imperil themselves but also diminish love of neighbor. (GRA VI, 436)

The Christian populace fails its contemporaries if it postpones all protest until a state becomes so corrupt that revolution seems the only course of action. (PED, 100)

The social commandments of the law remain ideally normative for a stable society and for civil government, whether in ancient pagan Rome or in modern secular America. Paul instructs Christians in Rome not to fear the ruler's power but to merit his praise by the practice of love that eschews murder, adultery, theft, false witness and coveting. (TGC, 71-72)

There is no doubt that the Bible obliges even pagan rulers to exercise power according to God's law, for as avengers of God's wrath the authority of God's ordinances stands behind them. The magistrate is himself subject to criticism and divine judgment for lawlessness. But to contend that all Old Testament ethical instruction, including the very penal sanctions enforced by the Hebrew theocracy, provides the judicial norm for every modern society is highly questionable. (GRA VI, 447)

To impose the death penalty as a currently necessary response of civil government to idolatry and apostasy, sorcery and witchcraft, adultery or unchastity, sodomy and bestiality, homosexuality and rape and incest, sabbath-breaking, blasphemy and false prophesying, and children who curse father or mother, has no evident New Testament basis. (GRA VI, 448)

Since New Testament times, God has willed the dispersion of believers throughout the politically pluralistic nations for the sake of world witness and service. The Old Testament reveals not only the universal principles of social ethics but also stipulates specific legislation for the theocracy. Some of that legislation may have value beyond the Old Testament, but not on a covenant-nation basis. The alternative to theocracy is not secular political relativism, unbridled self-interest, and military expansionism. (L)

Over and above affirming the legitimacy of civil government for the stipulated objectives of preserving peace and order, the Bible, on the basis of a divine command morality, sets forth certain enduringly valid social principles. It does not, however, set forth the detailed particularities of statute law for pluralistic governments as it did for the Old Testament theocracy. In a pluralistic society legislation is not based on theocratically and bureaucratically imposed spiritual and ethical beliefs championed as the public duty of all citizens by one of several community components. (CMSS, 112-13)

The devout man must respect law, and he is spiritually inclined to obey the positive law of the State. But the Christian's duty involves not simply the observance of those statutes which seem to strengthen the Decalogue. Nor is it the Christian view to condition one's support of the State upon its promotion of Christian religious principles, and to withhold support unless the State operates on explicitly sectarian principles. . . . The political order does not exist for the enforcement of sectarian objectives. (ACSE, 79-80)

Politics

Nowhere does the New Testament provide the institutional church any authority, jurisdiction, or mandate to wield direct pressure upon government and public agencies for commitment to specific ecclesiastically approved policies and programs. (PED, 46-47)

The Bible . . . doesn't tell you whether to go ahead with nuclear energy or not, or to build a certain bomb or not. But it gives you principles. And in the light of those principles, we seek the preferable alternative among the various live options available. Now that may seem very distressing to the person who wants only absolutes and thinks it's a waste of time to deal with probability. But life in the political order is like that, and in the political order we are not bringing in the kingdom of God. (E2)

Political action does not lend itself to a hurried implementation of the millennium; in truth, it is not a means to the millennium at all. (CCDC, 136)

The Bible gives no blueprint for a universal evangelical political order. (CT)

The New Testament is not . . . a book of political models. It does not approve any one form of government—whether monarchy, republic or democracy—as ideal, although it does exclude tyranny. The New Testament assumes the legitimate existence of divergently formed nations. (CMSS, 133)

Fortunately, the American founding fathers did not equate representative government with Christianity, as if religious sanction exists exclusively for this one political system. (ACSE, 90)

Scattered as they are throughout all the nations of the world, Christians more than ever before live under a great variety of governments as a result of the political upheavals of our generation. Their opportunities and methods of political action differ widely, as do their relationships to legislative processes. Someone like myself, who believes that the representative form of government has much to commend it, even that it incorporates political virtues and blessings to an exceptional degree, must nonetheless guard against overadulating or uncritically supporting some particular form of government. (ACSE, 73)

Christians should pray for rulers and for national righteousness, be exemplary citizens, promote justice in public affairs, and serve with integrity in public office as opportunity arises. (L)

Biblical revelation confines itself largely to ideal principles of social order; it does not commit itself to particular parties or programs of social reform. A serious approach to political responsibilities, however, must move from the norms or principles to involvement with personalities, parties, and programs in the given situation, and must grapple with their respective claims to serve the cause of justice and truth. (ACSE, 129)

Instead of seeking political power, the churches should delineate and promote the proper use of power. . . . To take the route of a Christian party is, in my view, a mistake. But neither is it right to commit oneself unreservedly to one of the existing parties. (CT)

If there is a Christian party, the churches will inherit the blame for all political failure of that party. (L)

A cohesive strategy requires some pattern of party involvement. It is at this point that evangelicals are often paralyzed because of their sense of evangelistic priority and their repudiation of ecumenical forces that politicize the Christian message and the church. They are right, of course, in fearing ecclesial abuse of power; they are wrong, however, in allowing such possible abuse to discourage Christians from public involvement. In political matters evangelicals have not learned the strategy of probing shared or coordinated perspectives and goals and methods. . . . (GRA VI, 441)

Either American evangelicals will align themselves in coalition on certain political objectives that they share in common or there will be evangelical collapse, conflict, and chaos in their political stance, and the last state of their involvement will be worse than their earlier noninvolvement. (L)

Many Christians are reluctant to engage in political affairs because they feel they should concern themselves only with changeless absolutes. But in a pluralistic society legislation is essentially a matter of compromise; in the absence of a clear majority consensus, the political outlook is shaped by coordinating coalitions that share common concerns. (CMSS, 126)

Evangelicals need to learn that political action, even when it falls within governmental authority, is often a matter of doing what seems right at the time in view of biblical teaching and available empirical data, but also of being prepared to make later revisions and even reversals in the light of additional information. While the biblical framework may often have theological support for some particular decision, it does not give us ready-made answers for all legislative situations. (GRA VI, 442)

In reaching a decision on specific economic issues, it is often exasperatingly difficult to say that *this* is the Christian position. Too often such decisions must be made within a framework of political and economic institutions which themselves can hardly be reconciled with biblical principles. (ACSE, 136)

Law

Many social problems today arise as much from attaching extravagant expectations to legislative reforms as from misuse of political power. Doubtless each proposed reform has something to commend it to the public—not least of all, the sincerity of its proponents and the existence of some social evil that needs correction. But political compulsion does not automatically produce "good" people, who, obviously, are an indispensable ingredient of a good society. (ACSE, 109)

Almost all legislative issues end up involving a moral choice. All legislation reflects a moral judgment and impinges on conduct. (CMSS, 112)

The appeal to public reason in political disputation does not preclude the Church from affirming on appropriate occasions that its moral absolutes derive from special divine revelation. Such occasions arise when civil government requires Christians to act contrary to the revealed will of God; when the Church is requested to testify to its position on special issues in legislative hearings; and when the Church as Church sets itself against intractable injustice in the sociopolitical context. (TGC, 34)

If we completely isolate the political arena from moral absolutes we inevitably condemn it to moral relativism. (CMSS, 112)

Christians cannot hope to reshape the world by political crusades; they must address attitudes and motives as well as structures. (CMSS, 128)

The Apostle Paul was fully aware that the Roman State was not a "Christian government." Yet in Romans 13:9 he adduces the prohibition of adultery, murder, covetousness, and stealing on the apparent premise that the second table of the Decalogue—that is, the social aspect of the law—is somehow anticipated by the conscience of all persons as part of the created givenness of humanity. These precepts speak of the inviolability of human life, of preservation of the integrity of family life, and of property rights—principles that today are under aggressive attack. (CMSS, 108)

While Hebrew judicial law supplied a political constitution that expounded rules of justice and equity, it lacked the perpetual authority of the moral law; other nations were free to adopt their own laws (without regard to Israel's political constitution or judicial law), but on the basis of the moral law as summarized in the Ten Commandments. . . . The Apostle Paul in Romans 13:8-10 instructs the early Christians that they will best avoid punishment at the hands of pagan rulers by keeping the social laws of the Decalogue. (ACSE, 98)

Christians are less than faithful to Christ's lordship over all political concerns if they imply that no moral choices flow from Christ's lordship in matters of political decision. (CMSS, 126)

The weakness of the view that the majority will determine the content of legislation is that while it suspends on a majority vote the validity of the Christian or any other view of what is right, it provides no criterion for judging and assessing that consensus. A majority—even a majority of Americans—can be wrong. (CMSS, 120)

Whoever considers the politico-economic status quo sacred or normative, or uncritically resigns himself to it, needs to reread the Scriptures. (TGC, 65)

Political Activism

Evangelicals by and large have neglected a comprehensive policy of socio-political and cultural involvement and have tended instead to get in only on specifics. (PJ)

Evangelical political activism imported a sense of evangelistic urgency into the political arena. But it lacked an articulate covering philosophy of political involvement and a comprehensively coordinated strategy. For one thing, the ecumenical political left, with its lingering social gospel enthusiasms, collapsed more quickly than expected. For another, the style of evangelical public involvement has been protest more than theory. This left the effort vulnerable to ambiguity in bridging from biblical imperatives to specific political commitments, and even to conflicting and rival priorities. (CMSS, 98)

The current tendency is to mobilize church opinion for civil disobedience and mob pressures even where avenues of persuasion have not been exhausted. (PED, 49)

Given a comprehensive vision and theology of politics illumined by scriptural principles, God's people have the task of translating these into policies and platforms and support for desirable programs and candidates. (CT)

Effective political involvement begins at the precinct level. (L)

Christians should be the champions, first and foremost, of freedom, especially in an age of totalitarian tyranny. They should be seen not simply as promoters of a particular political and religious agenda, but as champions of the rights of all humans under God, as advocates of liberty to act according to the will of God rather than submit to the arbitrary demands of rulers or even the preferences of a majority of fellow citizens. (L)

Freedom is comprehensive and indivisible in principle; it cannot be fragmented without jeopardy to the whole. (CMSS, 73)

The prime political issue of this century is liberty. Liberty under God, to be sure, but liberty nonetheless. The prophets of freedom are dwindling. That is why we hear more about peace than about liberty and the moral responsibility to deter predator powers. (CMSS, 10)

The alternatives are clear: either we return to the God of the Bible or we perish in the pit of lawlessness. (GRA VI, 454)

HISTORY

The exodus from Egypt, the founding of the Hebrew nation, the crucifixion and resurrection of Jesus Christ, and the founding of the Christian church are not simply internal spiritual perspectives; they are historically factual occurrences, and in truth the very cornerstone of history when seen in comprehensive context. (GRA I, 163-64)

Not only does the God of the Bible reveal himself in history, but the very idea of history takes its rise from biblical religion. (GRA II, 312)

The Christian derives his philosophy of history not by examining isolated events or from internal impressions, but from the Bible, that is, from divinely inspired writers who convey God's revealed purpose in human affairs. (GRA II, 320)

That God accomplishes his sovereign purposes in history is affirmed by the Pentateuch and by the Gospels, by the prophets and by the apostles. The Old Testament writers refer repeatedly to God's activity in history, the Gospels speak of God's providential and redemptive involvement in the world. From the Christian standpoint any denial that God is sovereignly active in history reflects a basic departure from the classic texts. (GRA II, 258)

The Bible affirms that the unity of human history lies in the moral and spiritual purpose of God who punishes sin and rewards righteousness. (RB)

Orthodox theism has nothing in common with a faith that sacrifices either sound historical method or intellectual honesty. (GRA II, 311)

Evangelical Christianity insists that certain specific historical acts are integral and indispensable to Judeo-Christian revelation. (GRA II, 311)

Ours is a world of staggering changes in which great nations like Britain topple from world supremacy, sleeping nations like China stir themselves awake, and new nations like Israel rise from the dust of past ages. . . . It is a world in which man has learned to walk in outer space without cosmic dizziness, halt the advent of human life with a capsule, postpone death by a heart transplant, and commute to the moon. . . . But it is also a runaway world in which totalitarian dictators destroy human dignity and rights openly, while the democracies do the same things in more subtle ways. Ours is a world in which war has not only gone global but has also taken to the heavens, in which man has split the atom and treated populous cities like Hiroshima to cremation. It is a world running from the random past into a computerized future. Restless of restraints and running from God, it is a world on rampage, a world gone radical, rebellious, and renegade, and a world resistant to divine authority. (NSF, 94-95)

No more remarkable disregard of empirical history is found today than the communist faith that a truly free society will inevitably arise from the Marxist ideology, despite the fact that none of the two dozen socialist societies fulfills that prospect and almost all are dictatorial and totalitarian. (GRA VI, 476)

We should remind humanist critics that world history records no persecution and inhumanity more debased and cruel than that waged against theists and dissenters under the banner of atheistic philosophies and rulers. Examples include the Hitler regime's murder of six million Jews and vast numbers of Gentiles, Stalin's destruction of some fifteen million Russians, and Mao's approved murder of some twenty-five million Chinese. (CCDC, 17)

God's purposes and Christ's kingdom are invincible. God has sovereignly so disposed the course of the universe and of history that even the severest hostility to his will instrumentally displays and promotes his sovereignly redemptive plan. God himself guarantees that eternal hell will subordinate the powers of evil and subjugate the impenitent wicked, that unreconciled freedom will not forever frustrate love, and that ultimately the created universe will be totally in the service of righteousness. (GRA V, 330)

Creation looks to a grand climax, one that first supplements creation with a history, but then in turn brings that history to an end by adding something eternal to the history. (GRA VI, 494)

Neither historical analysis nor political prediction can guarantee the future, which God controls. The Bible speaks of regathered Israel; there is no express mention of America, Japan and other great modern powers. Two dramatic tracks of world history are unfolding, one secular, the other spiritual, although this contrast must not be overdrawn or overstated. There is the drama of the United Nations with its massive global power blocs, and the drama of the Middle East, where God has regathered dispersed Israel—in unbelief, as the Bible forewarns—and where all those long-forgotten once-great powers of the past are being resurrected from the dust to world prominence—Iran, Saudi Arabia, Iraq, Syria, Lebanon, with Russia poised virtually at their borders. (RB)

This biblical insistence, that history moves to a goal, is the great Hebrew-Christian conviction which influential modern non-biblical philosophies have infused into their systems, without taking also the biblical metaphysics within which the conviction can alone be sustained. (NDG, 128)

The clock has notched closer to the midnight hour for evangelical destinies in our century. (FAF, 177)

The final chapter of history is not in human hands. (PD, 10)

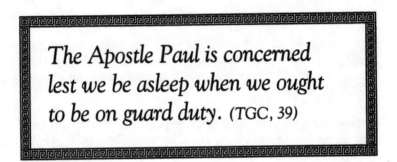

The Apostle Paul is concerned lest we be asleep when we ought to be on guard duty. (TGC, 39)

HOLY SPIRIT

The apostles taught that a life unfilled by the Spirit degrades authentic Christianity; only a life filled by the Spirit preserves the divine intention that man live in full spiritual and moral fellowship with his Creator. However diversely the theological community may evaluate the charismatic movement today, the fact remains that many Christian churches have too long obscured the Holy Spirit's person and work, and that recovery of the doctrine and reality of the Spirit by the community of faith is spiritually imperative. (GRA VI, 370)

Where the Holy Spirit is not the empowering agent of ethical effort, where he is neglected or excluded, the result is either a mottled morality that cannot fully claim to be Christian, or a grafting of some features of Christian behavior on an essentially unregenerate man. (CPE, 442)

Christ's substitutionary death, resurrection and glorification were preconditions for the Spirit's comprehensive ministry. (GRA VI, 374)

Not only do all Christians experience the Holy Spirit as a precondition of personal regeneration, not only are all believers baptized with the Spirit into the body of Christ at the time of their regeneration, but the Holy Spirit also permanently indwells all believers. (GRA, 386)

The fullness of the Spirit is to be maintained daily throughout the Christian life. Nowhere does the New

Testament exhort those who are already believers to seek the baptism of the Spirit, but it does exhort them to seek the continual filling of the Spirit since the fullness of the Spirit is not a once-for-all-time permanent gift. (GRA VI, 386)

Modernist theology reduced the Spirit of God from a distinct person to a divine power or influence. (GRA IV, 256)

The carping comment that the Holy Spirit has been gagged by evangelicals, who emphasize the completion of the canon, is an outright caricature. The far larger danger is that human beings will snap a lock on the Bible. (GRA IV, 283)

The true and living God has had from the very first a far higher goal than evangelical recovery of the inerrant autographs, or the writing of his law upon stone and scroll; his ultimate goal is to etch his Word fully upon the hearts of believers. (GRA IV, 242)

The Spirit's fullness is connected with a considerable diversity of gifts, all bestowed for the edification of the whole body of believers. (GRA VI, 388)

The risen Christ's power is evident among multitudes of humans whose lives radiate with joy, spiritual vitality, moral earnestness, inner peace, and outgoing love in a melancholy age. All around us we see the frightful cheapness and shocking vulgarity of modern human existence, the hollow reason and numbed conscience of those who refuse to think about God, and the warped consolation drawn from the illusion that we are but pebbles lashed by the chaotic winds of change-ridden history. (BPP)

The decline of joy as a spiritual possession today in contrast with primitive Christianity is due to some imperfection in the Christian life. (CPE, 495)

Despite the moral and spiritual gloom of our times, Christians have every reason for hope and high courage.

Why should we allow the world to cast its pall upon us? No segment of humanity has more joy, more moral power, more inner peace, more enduring hope for the future than those of every race and nation who have come to know Christ. It is high opportunity time for a bold sharing of good news. (CMSS, 48)

Our generation consumes huge quantities of sedatives, barbiturates, and other tranquilizers in mute testimony to its haunting anxieties. . . . Before our age of so-called miracle medicines a noted Bible commentator translated the Isaian reference to "the Prince of Peace" to read "the Tranquilizer." Jesus offered his disciples peace such as he knew on the way to crucifixion—and it wasn't a prescription for Valium. (C)

JESUS CHRIST

The great distinctive of Christianity is the person and work of Jesus Christ who lifts the whole conception of divine revelation to a new order. (WT)

Anyone who has pursued doctoral studies in theology or philosophy knows how seldom the private life of founders of influential speculative systems and of great world religions is considered at all relevant, even when weighed by those systems or religions. Contemporary moralists write lengthy textbooks without a single reference to Jesus of Nazareth. Yet of whom can it be said as of the Nazarene that in him the Word truly became flesh? (CCDC, 24)

Jesus claimed to be the singular Son of God. If he was self-deceived, we can hardly credit his lesser claims about God's purposes and commands. The Gospels deny that he was a mere man, even the superlatively good man. The New Testament alternatives reduce to the God-man or to a blasphemer and deceiver. These alternatives divided those who crucified him and those who worshiped him. (WT)

Buddhism promises to lead one to cessation of individual selfhood, and other religions tell us where they propose to lead us. Jesus Christ promises to lead us into the presence of the Father, and he will make good on his promise. (BPP)

The controversy over the person of Christ turns repeatedly through the centuries on much the same issues, so that one need only exchange names and times and places in the history of unbelief. (GRA III, 105)

Were we to discard the guideposts furnished by the ecumenical creeds and to return to the sacred Scriptures alone for our estimate of the God-Man, it would not be long before once again we would be involved in church councils and find ourselves confronted by the problems which gave Nicea and Chalcedon no rest until they had affirmed the full deity and full humanity of Christ. (PD, 207)

From the left came the attack of humanism, which claimed to apply consistently the half-hearted appeal which liberalism had made to the scientific method. If evangelicalism clarified the fact that liberalism had not taken the Christian records in earnest, humanism made it equally clear that liberalism had not taken empirical methodology, in the name of which it had renounced miraculous revelation and fiat creation, seriously either. If liberalism appealed to the absoluteness or finality of Jesus, it did so at the expense of scientific tentativity. . . . The inherent logic of the liberal position involved a move to the left, at least to humanism, and not a half-hearted appeal both to the Bible and to science, which amounted actually, in the sight of the humanists, to an inconsistent fundamentalism. (FYPT, 64-65)

Whatever may be said about him, whether as a teacher or as a redeemer, his sinlessness is unique in the stream of human life. Nowhere does history show a fountain of righteousness like the ethical pureness which ever lives in him. He presented the ideal of the Kingdom not merely in word but in deed and fact. He is the word of truth and of goodness become flesh. What he taught he uncompromisingly exemplified. (CPE, 399)

We need to chafe under the Savior's example—the lives he touched, the way he spent his days, the security he found in God. His portfolio carried no heavenly investment in the perpetuity of the Roman Empire or even in the real estate of Palestine. (CMSS, 21)

What Jesus taught his disciples was to put God first and to subsume all else under him—*everything*: Caesar, survival, money, status, power, everything. Caesar has his place, but there is one Lord, the Lord Jesus Christ; survival has its place, but he that clings to physical life above all other values betrays eternal perspectives; mammon has its place, but love of money is a root of evil; other things have their place as well, but life's true fullness does not consist of an infinity of sex, of status, or of things. (CCDC, 43)

In a day when God is caricatured by the crude images of our callous culture, Jesus Christ perfectly preserves and perpetuates the divine image. In a day when impersonal processes—quarks and quasars—are given primacy, Jesus Christ stands as the first-born of all creation and the sovereign creator of all things and powers. In a day when humanism considers history and nature haphazard, purposeless, and directionless, Christ remains the upholding and unifying principle of the universe which exists through him and for him. In a day when the world is crammed with evil, the fullness of the Godhead dwells in Jesus Christ who stands in incomparable relationships both to the Godhead and to the universe. The divine essence is his; he precedes the universe in time and surpasses it in rank; he is the agent in its creation and the sustainer of it; he supplies its unity and meaning, and is its final goal. (CCDC, 90)

The fixed center of interest in the divine Name now becomes Jesus of Nazareth, the promised Deliverer, the incarnate and exalted Lord. More than a hundred names and titles are applied to him, all of which blend into one in eternity. (GRA II, 245-46)

When Christianity speaks of the new man, it points first and foremost to Jesus of Nazareth. (GRA IV, 522)

Without question, the best known fact about Jesus Christ is that he gave the Sermon on the Mount. People may not have the vaguest notion of what the Sermon on the Mount is all about, but they invariably connect "Jesus Christ" with "The Sermon on the Mount" and add what a "good thing" they think it is. Actually it is his fullest treatment of morality. (CPE, 278)

Jesus Christ is not only the proclaimer of a divinely given Word, but also, on the basis of his inherent divine authority, himself stipulates and determines the Word of God. The prophetic formula "the Word of the Lord came unto me" is replaced on Jesus' lips by "But I say unto you." (GRA II, 11)

Not only did Jesus criticize scribal modification of the Old Testament, not only did he find the deepest significance of the law and the prophets in his own messianic identity, not only did he claim singular divine authority to define the precise intention of the inspired writers, but he also inaugurated the promised "new covenant" with moral power to transcend the Old Testament ethical plateau. (GRA III, 41)

God reveals his nature not in intelligible propositions alone or only in miraculous deeds; he reveals himself supremely in Jesus Christ, whose life and death and resurrection are cognitively and propositionally interpreted by the inspired Scriptures. (GRA V, 16)

Important as was the role of the apostles, none of them claims to be a divine-human mediator in the absolute sense. (GRA III, 59)

Only the gospel of Christ's mediatorial work can turn sinful man's expectation of coming judgment into an ardent eschatological hope, one that longs for "the ages to come." (GRA III, 73)

Death and Resurrection

That rude cross outside Jerusalem becomes the central reference point of history; the divine purpose in the beginning of time, and the divine issue at the end of time, can be understood aright only within the biblical conviction that this gift of God's Son stands indeed as the fulfillment of time. And this gift, purchasing for us temporal creatures the gift of eternal life, discloses at the same time the divine purpose for redeemed humanity, which is to bring man more and more into the image of Christ Jesus. Here time is treated not alone seriously, but with a perilous and awful seriousness; each moment is a rendezvous with the God who is supreme over time, who is the sovereign Lord of history. (NDG, 135)

To develop the doctrine of God in biblical terms is to speak inevitably of Jesus Christ, and to speak of Him not simply by way of preface but by way of climax. (GWSH, 5)

The rise of the Christian movement can be adequately explained in only one way, that Jesus' followers personally saw the risen Lord and considered his resurrection from the tomb conclusive evidence that he was truly the Messiah of Old Testament promise. (GRA III, 147)

From the technically qualified representatives of the Hebrew Sanhedrin, from the military watch officially surrounding and guarding the grave of the entombed crucified Jesus—from them the God of history in his divine providence elicited the candid, unreserved confession and open acknowledgment that the tomb was empty. (GRA III, 150)

Two lines of testimony come from the enemies of the Christian movement: First, the Sanhedrin was forced to acknowledge the empty tomb because of and through its officially designated representatives who were stationed in round-the-clock operations at the scene of action. Second, the Sanhedrin must have been stunned when Saul, its official investigator and persecutor, repudiated the notion that the disciples had stolen the crucified body and became instead a worshiper and servant of the risen Jesus even, as it developed, to the death, and moreover exhorted all Jewry and the whole Gentile world to worship him. (GRA III, 154)

That the biblical writers date the resurrection after Jesus' burial and not simultaneously with His death indicates they meant bodily resurrection, not merely soul survival. (NSF, 71)

Many may think the Christian religion has run its course, and that the gloom of Good Friday is now settling over the long history of the church. But they are wrong. The reality of the resurrection cannot so easily be undone. In truth, it is the world of unbelief that remains on notice of judgment. (FAF, 36)

Jesus' resurrection was no bizarre contingency that defied human logic. It was not an utterly incoherent incursion into history. However unique and unparalleled as a historical event, the resurrection of Jesus Christ took place in a coherent framework of meaning. Its context stretched back far beyond the events of Passion Week. (NSF, 68)

The New Testament does not exhibit Jesus' resurrection as merely a prelude to some distant future. For regenerate believers, the resurrection is a present reality known and anticipatively experienced in daily fellowship with the risen Jesus. From the ascended Christ his followers received the indwelling Spirit outpoured at Pentecost; so too they still receive from him the Spirit's daily filling, and by the Spirit taste even now the powers of the age to come and are daily sampling their coming inheritance. (GRA III, 163)

The only human nature God applauds and singularly promoted into the eternal future is that of Jesus Christ, the perfect Son of God. God has not raised from the dead Pontius Pilate or Herod or Caiaphas, who must wait their day; he has not even raised Augustine or Luther or Calvin or Wesley, not even Moses or John the Baptist or the apostle Paul, but Jesus only. . . . Nobody but Jesus has marched into the world of death and defanged it, marched through it and left it in disarray, stripped away its sting and triumphed over it. (CCDC, 98)

The three years of Jesus' public ministry have stimulated more comment and literature across nineteen centuries than any other comparable segment of human history. (PED, 55)

The bunny, colored eggs and jelly beans are so much confetti. Easter is Jesus Christ or it is nothing. (WT)

Most academics studiously avoid classroom reference to Jesus Christ—understandably so: for to mention Christ in a formative way would only put intellectual and moral world-wisdom on the defensive. (CH)

The Jesus movement expressed evangelical fidelity not by affirming the Apostles' Creed but by shouting Jesus cheers ("Give me a J! Give me an E!. . ."). (GRA I, 126)

No story, from disaster to delight, stands out above the day I came to know Jesus Christ and the forgiveness of sins, came to be on speaking terms with God, and came to find a sense of high direction and holy meaning in life. (FAF, 69-70)

We must preach Jesus Christ, who makes evangelical experience possible. People in the pews may thirst for some morsel of evangelical gossip or for some biographical tidbit; they may even expect a bit of name-dropping, or want to hear the worst about some backsliding evangelical effort. But we are to give centrality to the Name that is above every other name. (CCDC, 93)

Christ speaks of true freedom, of being free indeed. Free, period. Free, exclamation point! No tricks, no small print.

Christ's freedom is simply and purely freedom, FREEDOM in capital letters. There is no real freedom except the freedom that God offers and provides. (CCDC, 68)

The risen Christ is in the moving and lifting business. How far has He removed you from the old life and lifted you to divine service? How high has Christ lifted you? (TGC, 42)

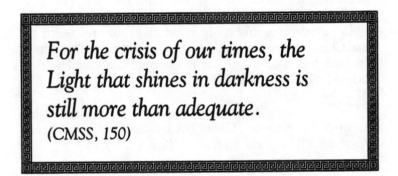

For the crisis of our times, the Light that shines in darkness is still more than adequate.
(CMSS, 150)

JUSTICE

Authentic faith and a commitment to righteousness/justice go hand in glove. (TGC, 30)

Scripture unequivocally affirms the future final triumph of justice and the decisive defeat of unrighteousness. (GRA VI, 419)

The Bible views social injustice as a matter of apostasy from the living God; it issues from false conceptions of duty that deny Yahweh to be truly Lord. (GRA VI, 438)

A civil government truly devoted to justice will reflect at least two basic concerns: first, that its civil laws conform to the constitutional guarantees that span successive regimes and thus provide a relatively objective standard of justice, and second, that its constitutional criteria conform to transcendent criteria that will ultimately judge all rulers and constitutions. In fallen history no political document can be presumed to fully elucidate what divine justice implies. (GRA VI, 422)

Notably divergent claims in behalf of justice made by the great religions of the modern world leave little doubt that their conflict over the definition and content of justice is basically a conflict between rival conceptions of deity through whom or which justice is perceived. This fact is evident from the divergent claims that stem from biblical justice, modern permissive liberal justice, atheistic communism and nonbiblical religions. The modern world knows only too well that defining the content of justice is among today's most urgent and volatile concerns: the detailed content of justice is obviously not self-evident. (GRA VI, 428)

The very definition of justice is up for grabs today as it has not been since New Testament times. For starters, there is biblical justice, Communist justice, modern liberal Western justice (which the Khomeini regime denounces as tolerant of sexual permissiveness and other vices), Shiite justice (which many Iranian revolutionaries who helped to enthrone it must now wish they could escape), and Islamic justice generally. (TGC, 28)

Fundamental to biblical theology is the revelation of the true and living God, the God both of justice and of justification. (PED, 120)

The clouding of divine justice soon deprives external justice of lucent transcendent supports. Human justice soon fades into special preferences for the powerful. (GRA VI, 417)

Rights

The modern controversy over human rights calls urgently for a theological recovery of the metaphysical foundations of these rights. Human rights are grounded in God's transcendent will for man made in his image. The basis of human rights is not supplied by positive law nor can these rights be reliably defined by analyzing human nature or human experience. (GRA VI, 426)

The Bible does not teach that human beings simply on the basis of existence have inherent or *a priori* rights, or that they have absolute rights accruing from sociological or political considerations. The Bible has a doctrine of divinely imposed duties; what moderns call human rights are the contingent flipside of those duties. (TGC, 148)

In the Christian view, inalienable rights are creational rights governing the community and individual, rights implicit in the social commandments of the Decalogue. The modern separation of rights from duties and from a divine ground encourages a ready misidentification of human needs as rights, since empirical observation of human nature yields conflicting versions of what is "natural" to humanity. (TGC, 158)

Current legal theory leaves in doubt not simply the identification of legitimate rights—a subject that currently preoccupies most juridical controversy—but a clear view also of what, if anything, constitutes legitimacy other than formal-legal validity. (TGC, 155)

However offensive to secular humanism, the theological referent gains double relevance through the conspicuous collapse of modern rights theories. It invests law with transcendent awe and objective authority, and it corresponds to the human condition through its explanation of the confusion over law's nature and content by the fact of moral rebellion. (TGC, 159)

What is widely overlooked today is that a world view based on naturalistic evolution can provide no reasonable foundation for either the universality or the permanence of human rights; it was precisely such naturalistic theory that underlay the Nazi repudiation of the inherited biblical morality of the West. (GRA VI, 152)

Justice is at home in heaven not only because God dwells there and will reign as king over the coming new heavens and new earth, but also because justice has its very foundation and essential structure in the kingdom of God. (GRA VI, 420)

Christians stand in the tradition of the holy prophets who proclaimed the justice of God and deplored injustice even at great personal risk. (GRA VI, 437)

Justice steps dramatically into fallen history in the holy person of Messiah, Jesus Christ. (GRA VI, 430)

Jesus applies to his own person and work the Isaian good news concerning the coming liberator and promised liberation. (GRA III, 68)

Jesus lived out Isaiah 61, inscribing that passage on messianic liberation over his public ministry (Luke 4:17ff), although he postponed beyond the present church age 'the day of vengeance' when the Lord will implement universal justice by transcendent force. By his sinless life Jesus triumphed over all the powers of evil, and by his bodily resurrection he vanquished all the oppressive and exploitative powers that would have destroyed him. Since his crucifixion and resurrection all the powers of injustice are dated and doomed. (CH)

Jesus Christ has already been unveiled as the sinless exalted Judge of mankind and the nations. (GRA VI, 433)

Poverty

Responding to destitution is not a duty of Christians only but of every man everywhere. The masses in the great centers of destitution—India, Pakistan, Bangladesh, Indonesia—are Buddhist, Hindu and Muslim. It is scandalous that petrol-rich Arab oil sheiks drop millions of dollars in a single night at the gaming tables in London, and that Hindu leaders oppose aid to the lowest caste as an attack on established religion, culture, and social stability. (L)

The vision of a present world-order without poverty was not present in Old Testament thought, or in ancient Graeco-Roman thought, or in New Testament thought, or in medieval Christian thought. The Bible teaches that God has a special eye for the destitute and that those who are entrusted with more than their needy neighbors have a duty to be compassionate. This duty is universal and devolves on non-Christians as well as Christians. But the Bible does not teach forced redistribution of wealth. (CCDC, 34)

God often uses wicked powers to punish other powers that have had more light, before he in turn destroys them; that holds awesome possibilities for America, Soviet Russia and mainland China also. It is still true that righteousness is the best guarantee to national survival; military might can hold off predator powers but it does not guarantee the future. (RB)

In the coming judgment of modern unbelief, the ancient pagan Greeks will rise to witness against the great modern learning centers of Europe and the Anglo-Saxon West wherever our century sweeps away the supernatural, wherever it limits reality to the grid of empirical observation, wherever it sucks the whole of existence into the natural sciences, wherever it refers all the complex forms of life to natural evolution and natural selection and chance variation in a cosmic lottery,. wherever it reduces the ultimate world to impersonal processes and events and dismisses mind and personality and values as fate and accidental emergents in the flux of things. (CCDC, 111)

Revolution

If [a Christian] supports a revolutionary alternative to unjust structures and laws, he will do so mainly by stimulating respect for the righteous will of God which an unjust society tramples, rather than by fueling impatience, resentments and revolt. (PED, 104)

The Son of Man did not come to teach men to take up the sword for the cause of justice; rather, he offered men a new kind of life. (PED, 117)

Christians should not be anti-government but rather pro-justice. Thus they topple governments only indirectly, as government places itself in the service of injustice, although civil disobedience has apostolic precedent when the state requires the church to do what God forbids. (L)

Even if a government now and then exceeds its proper authority, the Christian's hope of a better tomorrow is sustained by a firm reliance on divine providence more than by enthusiasm for human revolution. (ACSE, 180)

Although not committed to revolution in principle, the Christian need not pledge his heart more than one day at a time to a regime whose attitudes toward the Church may be dictated simply by temporary strategy and whose eventual and permanent intentions are not clear. (ACSE, 186)

The strategy of revolution not only proposes to rectify social evils, but it denies the existence of divinely given structures in history and society. It would destroy and displace ultimate norms, whether in respect to marriage, property or the state. (ACSE, 17)

To speak of Christian impact as a "deeper" revolution, or as "genuine" revolution, is in fact dangerous. This way of describing the situation admittedly retains in principle a proper emphasis on the radical character of the Christian demand for a twice-born race of men. But it does not really come to grips with the Christian attitude toward the spirit of revolution rampant today. Moreover, it may encourage a misunderstanding of the Christian message in terms of mere political theory, and thereby also misrepresent the Christian Church's attitude toward secular government. (ACSE, 176)

The whole Christian heritage stands on the side of peaceful, legal, and orderly processes of change in society, rather than on the side of violence and revolution. (CT)

Christianity does not exist to guarantee felicitous survival to a world that insists upon rejecting God as the supreme source of its security. The Church is to be light, salt and leaven to the world, but it is not nor can it be salt that forever preserves a world indifferent to the light. (TGC, 31-32)

Christians may and must work with non-Christians anywhere and everywhere in mutual quest and pursuit of social justice. (PED, 68)

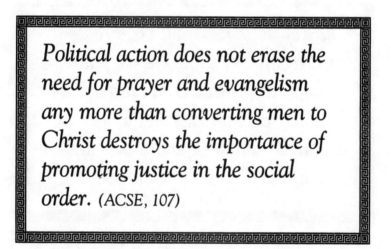

Political action does not erase the need for prayer and evangelism any more than converting men to Christ destroys the importance of promoting justice in the social order. (ACSE, 107)

Our religious neutrality is threatened whenever someone we know well takes spiritual commitment seriously and refuses any longer to play hide-and-seek and touch-and-go with the living God. (CCDC, 50)

KINGDOM OF GOD

According to the Synoptic Gospels, what best summarizes the whole of Jesus' teaching is this theme of the kingdom or rule of God. Jesus instructed his disciples to make it their main concern. (CCDC, 25)

Jesus preached the imminent coming of that kingdom; it was "at hand" in history; it was dawning in His own ministry, and His life and work revealed it as a present fact. (GWSH, 102)

He came to offer us a place in His Kingdom, and through the obedient devotion of twice-born men to show the power and authority of the king from age to age. (GWSH, 102)

While the New Covenant cannot be depicted as disinterested in just social legislation and structures, the Kingdom of God has transcendent eschatological and spiritual-moral features absent from secular utopian expectations. (PED, 92)

Not all Old Testament ethics is meant for today. The Hebrew theocracy is gone, along with the laws that were reserved for it, including the death penalty for adulterers, for incest, for sodomy, for perjury, for witchcraft, for abusing parents, for blasphemy, for Sabbath-breaking, for false teaching, for sacrificing to false gods. Capital punishment for murder, on the other hand, has a pre-theocratic status. We are to follow the lead of the New Testament in what is carried forward from the Old. (TGC, 30)

Christians today are dispersed worldwide as a new regenerate society and live amid a variety of political contexts, none of them a theocracy. Talk of the status of America as a Christian nation should not imply that the United States is a covenant nation standing in the same theocratic relationships to God as did the ancient Jewish state. (CMSS, 99)

Many Christians hold that a contemporary Christian government, one founded on theocratic principles, would be more harmful than helpful. When a supposedly Christian government's policy or program fails (for whatever reason) the Church is inevitably blamed. Will not Christians be disillusioned and in fact discredited if by political means they seek to achieve goals that the Church should ideally advance by preaching and evangelism? (COT, 394)

Instead of seeking to impose theocratic patterns upon society in general, the church is to be a christocracy over which Christ rules by the Scriptures. (CMSS, 107)

Biblical theology outlines quite other dynamisms than the church's use of force for approximating the Kingdom of God in fallen history. (PED, 100)

Where does the God of the New Testament utter a single endorsement of revolution as a human means or method of social change? Where does Jesus of Nazareth give his followers—even the clergy and theologians—the right to force Kingdom-structures upon the world? (PED, 99)

We have no mandate to theoretically legislate divine imperatives upon a pluralistic political realm. But we do have a duty to proclaim the revelatory truths and principles by which God will decisively judge every nation—and we must strive to advance them. If the ideas we affirm are spineless, if we bend biblical principles to accommodate one or another modern deviation, then what passes for evangelical behavior will soon obscure and even subvert revelatory perspectives and reinforce a sub-Christian society. (CCDC, 136-37)

God is King of the universe by his creation of it. He has power over all creatures as their creator and judge. The freedom he bestows on human creatures is determined by considerations that we ourselves neither create nor control: among them are the capacity to hear God's Word, the perilous alternatives of either faith or unbelief and of life either as God's servants or as mutinous rebels, and the high penalties of disobedience. Human self-determination is limited; we are free even as sinners to hear God's Word, but we are no longer free to do the good, and least of all to save ourselves. (GRA V, 318)

The fullness of His Kingdom will come at last not through man's self-effort but like lightning slashing from heaven. (GWSH, 103)

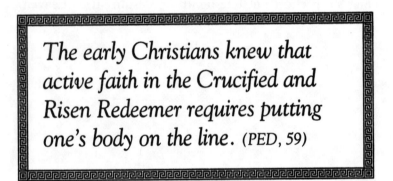

The early Christians knew that active faith in the Crucified and Risen Redeemer requires putting one's body on the line. (PED, 59)

LAST THINGS

Only one theological perspective, only one philosophical perspective, has an enduring future, a worldlife view, namely, that openly acknowledges that the future belongs to God. (GRA VI, 492)

Most secular philosophy lacks an eschatology; the question of endings is as much an embarrassment to it as the question of beginnings. (GRA VI, 492)

Whoever bids earnestly for the future must bid for big stakes. The living God is history's highest bidder and, awaiting the last trump, He has already bid the incarnation, the atonement, the resurrection and a small band of redeemed fishermen. (FAF, 37)

Christ conquered more than death. He conquered sin and death. It is this sinless, deathless future guaranteed by Christ's resurrection toward which God is moving us. (NSF, 73)

Through his substitutionary death and resurrection life, Jesus stands at the sluice-gates of eternity, and manifests God's holy sovereignty as the Lord of history and of the cosmos. (GRA III, 73)

No prophetic doctrine is more prominent in the New Testament than that of the promised personal return in great power and glory of the crucified, risen and now exalted Jesus.

The certainty of Christ's second coming the New Testament connects with the fact of his already accomplished first coming. (GRA VI, 498)

The dramatic and unmistakable message of the New Testament is that mankind lives already in the last days because of the resurrection of the crucified Messiah and that the very last of those days is now soon to break upon us. (GRA III, 20)

The intellectual idolatries are many, all the more because they are cherished by those who have no patience with revealed religion, fixed truths, eternal commandments. The one 'unthinkable' prospect of our technological society is (not the possibility of scientific destruction of modern civilization, for that prospect would congratulate the power potential of the scientific community, but rather) *divine doom!* The Second Coming of Christ, the End of all ends, the gates of hell, the resurrection of the dead, the final judgment of mankind—these are ruled out by the wisdom of the world. . . . So there arises a herd of humanity that anesthetizes the possibilities of spiritual life and knifes itself to spiritual death, a generation with mustard-seed consciences, a society that believes in pseudo-values and pseudo-truths. (CH)

The dilemmas that confound our leaders actually tell us much about the stupidities of our civilization with its moral facades and spiritual evasions. Military preparedness may indeed be a necessary deterrent in an age of predator powers. But any nation that thinks God may be tempted to evaporate because of this vast armory of destructive might has in store a mighty surprise when resurrection morning unveils that omnipotent judge of the nations. (CH)

The last time you read of Pontius Pilate in the New Testament, two prominent Christians are begging the pagan Roman governor for the body of Jesus. The next time world rulers and kings see the body of Jesus will be on the coming judgment day when all will bow the knee to the King of kings and Lord of Lords. (CCDC, 100)

For all the current Western emphasis on human self-determination, much of the modern world remains captive to deterministic views of reality and life. World leaders increasingly ask whether human history may not perhaps be ruled by alien forces that even the most powerful nations cannot contain or control. (GRA VI, 79)

Thousands pursue astrology on the premise that man and his world are governed by the stars. (GRA VI, 80)

Neither the United States nor the United Nations, neither the Communists nor the capitalists, neither scientists nor philosophers nor sociologists nor educators nor psychiatrists nor any other creature can offer anything more than a delaying action for doomsday. (NSF, 88)

Decision-time is over. Accounting-time has come. The pagan who said that there is no fixed truth, no final good, that man is a soulless beast and that purpose and meaning are private illusions, and that God is myth, stands for judgment at last before the one true and living God, the moral Lord of the universe, the Chief Justice and Arbiter of human destiny. (TGC, 61)

Our world and every last man in it have been placed on emergency alert. The coming Judge of our race is at hand, and all eyes shall soon behold the sent Son of God. (GRA III, 27)

God executes judgment not simply within history but climactically and finally at the end of history. The inspired writers tell us authoritatively not only what God is saying and doing now in nature and in history, but also give us intimations of what he will say and do when he consummates all things. (GRA II, 334)

During his earthly ministry Christ, *Agape* incarnate, repeatedly coupled reference to declarations of his lordship with warnings that Hades awaits the impenitent. (GRA VI, 351)

Jesus' teaching makes it patently obvious that no correct view of final judgment can be elaborated that empties hell of its terrors and depicts God's last judgment as benevolent toward the impenitent and ungodly. (GRA VI, 352)

God's most awesome silence in eternity will be his silence toward the lost, a punitive and retributive silence reserved for the wicked who are not on speaking terms with him. (GRA IV, 596)

Belief in an afterlife flickered and faded as Western philosophy increasingly neglected biblical revelation. (GRA VI, 500)

The Jews comprehended eternal life in terms of the age to come: Jesus correlates the scriptural witness to life eternal with the biblical testimony to himself as life-giver. (GRA III, 32)

The first Christians held out no false hopes to their contemporaries. They never implied that the climax of human existence is to be attained in some social utopia or private paradise discoverable in earthly history. Men are made for a destiny in eternity. (FAF, 182)

New Testament Christians expected the climax of human felicity not in this earthly existence but in a blessed afterlife. (PED, 45)

The final vindication of divine providence is not completed in this earthly life but is consummated in an end-time reckoning that eternally rewards faithful obedience. (GRA VI, 461)

A Christian knows that he will not be engulfed by this earth and that the time approaches when one moves up from it. (RB)

Our obligation to speak is not lessened by our conviction of the imminent return of Christ. What if we rise tomorrow?—we are *here* today, and a global mission is here with us. (UCMF, 66)

Who knows but that, before this generation shall end, Christ shall return in power, to write the final chapter of rebellious earthly history? Or, if not . . . whether we are on the threshold of a modern Dark Ages, when the forces of naturalism shall rob life of significance and history of meaning? The options are all terrible in their portent today and, in the valley of decision, we least of all have the right to remain but spectators. *(FYPT, 93)*

LOVE

No treatment of the virtues our Lord taught is adequate which does not assign first place to love. Love is the fountain of the pure heart and the forgiving spirit. (CPE, 482)

Love is prized above the highest charismatic gifts; those miraculous endowments associated with the apostolic ministry are transient in themselves, and become worthless when love is absent. (CPE, 484)

Whereas the Greeks comprehended love—whether sensual or sublime—as *eros*, that is, as essentially one's quest for a value that compensates for an inner need or defect, the *agapē* of God confers on the unworthy an undeserved value or boon. *Agapē*, in short, is the incomparable love of the holy God for rebellious sinners whose only destiny would otherwise be unmitigated doom. (GRA VI, 342)

Yet to compress the biblical view of divine love solely into the term *agapē* can raise unnecessary misunderstanding. Some scholars have inferred, for example, that all terms for love except *agapē* are inappropriate to the God of the Bible; the fact is that Jesus in the Gospel of John uses the term *phileō* when he states that "the Father loves the Son" (John, 5:20, NIV), and does so as well when speaking of the Father's love of the disciples (John 16:27). . . . There have [been] efforts on the basis of John 21:15ff to press an exegetical distinction between *phileō* and *agapaō*; such attempts are now widely rejected, however, because the interpreters make conflicting

133

inferences, and because John frequently uses synonyms as a matter of literary style. (GRA VI, 343)

Christian love (*agapē*) is the antithesis of worldly hate, but it is much more; it is the antithesis also of worldly love (*eros*) in all its forms. The gods of our time are but brittle images of *eros*-love. (GWSH, 13)

Only through the impact of biblical religion does a truly significant conception of divine love in distinction from human love gain metaphysical significance in the ancient world. Neither classical mythology nor classical philosophy rises to a doctrine of a sovereign Creator who loves man and the world. (GRA VI, 340)

It can be demonstrated from the ancient as well as from the living religions of the world that, outside the biblical tradition, wherever the attributes of holiness and love are applied to deity, the application is such that either the divine love or the divine holiness is seriously compromised. The God of holy love, in the full meaning of that ascription, is the God who has revealed himself in the Scriptures, and that God alone. (NDG, 103)

Christian love is only half biblical when it deteriorates into a concern only for the souls of men and is indifferent to the needs of the body. What believer ministers to himself only in this way? It is scarcely biblical at all when it degenerates into a mere humanistic concern for the social side of life to the total neglect of the life of the spirit. (CPE, 231)

The revolt against the Logos is a revolt also against Agape, and the only genuine prototype of Agape is the Logos become flesh. (CPE, 142)

MAN

The Bible emphasizes the dignity and worth of every human life, yet emphasizes that physical survival is not the highest of all values. (WT)

Probably no terms have been more misused and misunderstood than the terms "human" and "manlike." (GRA VI, 197)

In the Bible what remains the determining constant of essential human nature is the presence in man at least in some respects of the divine likeness. (GRA VI, 197)

Whereas evolutionary study of man is preoccupied with man's likeness to the lower animals, the Genesis account speaks not at all about man's similarity to the other creatures; it delineates rather man's specially fashioned likeness to God. (GRA VI, 203)

The uniqueness of Adam lay not in his creation out of dust; animals and birds too had been fashioned out of the ground. But the fact that man names the animals attests his rule over them, and underscores their inability to serve as Adam's partner or helpmeet. (GRA VI, 240)

This intriguing phrase—the *imago Dei*—is not an archaic Latinism; it embraces the essential nature of man as he is on the basis of creation. (CPE, 151)

The image of God in man is sullied. Man is a moral rebel who is threatened by Divine wrath. (CPE, 172)

Fall of Man

The fall of man was a catastrophic personality shock; it fractured human existence with a devastating fault. Ever since, man's worship and contemplation of the living God have been broken, his devotion to the divine will shattered. . . . His revolt against God is at the same time a revolt against truth and the good; his rejection of truth is a rejection of God and the good, his defection from the good a repudiation of God and the truth. (GRA II, 135)

That Adam blamed Eve for this fall, is only part of the story; such shifting of responsibility anticipates the faceless "they" of society in general, a catchall mirage to which Adam's posterity still shunts the blame for sin and evil. (GRA VI, 247)

It was Hegelian philosophy which, a century ago, suggested that the event known traditionally as the "fall of man" should be an occasion for singing the Doxology, rather than for the provision of atonement. (PD, 125)

The perfectibility of man was thought to be a necessary implication of evolutionary philosophy. The biblical idea that man's nature includes a radical defect which inevitably undercuts the realization of his ideals and distorts his moral insights, was dismissed as unrealistic. (PD, 19)

The evolutionary philosophies furnished the modern mind with a cosmic guarantee of human perfectibility. (RMM, 62)

Throughout the western world, liberal religious thought substituted evolutionary sociology for biblical redemptionist anthropology as involving a method for solution of world problems which was assumed to be more rapid, more effective, and more scientific. (RMM, 64)

For evolutionists evil was but a remnant of brute instinct
in a world where emerging man gives content to the notions
of good and evil. The possibility follows, then, of eradicating
evil by mass education, bureaucratic socialization and technological revision of human nature. To consider man poten-
tially or essentially good upends the biblical view of sin.
(GRA VI, 259)

However proud man may be of his cultural achievements,
God is far less impressed by them. According to the Bible
human culture is under divine judgment; its glories are viti-
ated by the consequences of man's fall and spiritual rebellion.
(GRA VI, 228)

While the classic moral philosophers and founders of other
world religions teach that man may and should achieve moral
perfection by the gradual improvement of his present nature,
Christianity teaches, to the contrary, that only through the
atoning death of Christ and the regeneration and sanctification of the Holy Spirit is fallen man restored to fellowship
with his righteous Creator and to holiness. The sinner's
plight is such, says the Christian religion, that he needs supernatural rescue; in the terms of Scripture, he requires nothing
less than justification, regeneration and sanctification.
(GWSH, 78-79)

In revealing the world of human relations as a fallen world,
Hebrew-Christian ethics stresses the disparity between life as
it is and life as it ought to be. The world is in the grip of
Satan and his hosts. Man's fall and rebellion have darkened
the whole of human history with sin and death. The moral
law stands over against man as a threatening lawsuit. For one
reason only does the Bible proclaim the absolute necessity of
a "salvation ethics" centering in a Divine initiative. There
just is no other way out. (CPE, 187)

Man is his own greatest menace. . . . Only against the
backdrop of a contrary conviction which steadfastly absorbed

the loyalty of 350 years of modern philosophy can one feel the full force of the three syllables so often echoed in modern writing: "Man is sick." (RMM, 68-69)

On a mass scale, the value of human existence is almost totally discounted. The nadir of man's worth finds its supreme illustration not in the deeds of earlier centuries, but in those of our own: barbarism in Nazi concentration camps; brutal state compulsion under Soviet totalitarianism; slave labor camps; suspension of human rights upon the whim of political machines; scientific devotion to weapons efficient for wholesale death-dealing; mass atomic destruction of whole civilian populations (Nagasaki and Hiroshima) by world powers promoting the cause of human dignity. (CPE, 13)

Today the whole human family is staggered by massive problems, and man himself is the most conspicuous of them. (NSF, 15)

Numbers of our American cities are miring in savagery. With moral absolutes obscure if not disowned, young and old alike steep themselves in prurience and grovel in a shadow culture of drugs, drink and debauchery. Life for many people, as our great news magazines reflect it, has little meaning and purpose. Many now consider work distasteful, saving for the future unrewarding, reflective education a dispensable diversion, sport or travel our highest creative engagement, political protest the chief expression of democracy, and war a worse evil than loss of freedoms. (NSF, 119)

Nowhere in the creaturely world is there a more frustrated species than *homo sapiens*, and nowhere among man's many frustrations is his ineptness and incapacity more conspicuous than in respect to moral goals. (GRA I, 143)

One fact is certain: simultaneous with this relativity of moral imperatives, human life has lost its worth. The soul-nausea and dread of modern man has reached depths unknown even to the ancient Greek skeptic. The sense of cosmic lostness and of personal insignificance frames modern man's window on life. (CPE, 13)

The modern ideology needs to be remade—that is admitted today by those who have shaped it as well as those who have opposed it. But its effective remaking can be accomplished only in a philosophic framework in which rebirth is something more than a change of human temperament, in which indeed it is a divine reversal, a work of regeneration. If the modern mind is not reborn, but merely exchanges one mood for another, we stand only a generation from the fruit of atheism: the pessimism of despair. (RMM, 307)

Secular man does not miss out on general revelation, but he misses out on the joy of God and the goal of life. (GRA I, 151)

Evangelical Christianity insists that the long run of history discloses man's own inability to eliminate historical evil. But it emphasizes that there is an actual redemptive working of God in history, and that God achieves his redemptive purpose in part in the concrete historical situation. (PED, 53)

Youth

The young—more quickly than they suspect—are candidates for middle age and old age, and the precious twenties are gone like a summer night. Think of Jesus beginning his own public ministry just before he turned 30, choosing disciples from those in that age bracket, and enlisting them for an awesome world mission. What would He say to those for whose approbation politicians and professors aspire, flattering them by declarations of their incomparable importance to the modern world: "Don't deprive civilization of your potential!" Would Jesus not warn them of the house built on sand—and that their fondest dreams may well turn into a bag of wind? Would He not call them to refine their ideals and values—love, freedom, hope, happiness—lest they fall into the trap of irrational counterfeits? Would He not warn them against tradition—against the legacy that even many of their elders have left them? Would He not speak plainly of sin and shame and repentance and real life and freedom? Would He not warn them of the evils and temptations of society that have beguiled a parent generation, and that carry the youth generation in turn perilously near the gates of hell? . . . Would He not speak to them of liberating truth, power, love and joy, and enlist them, as He did Peter, John and James, in a world-wide mission that involves the destiny of all humans? (CH)

I detect a new longing by disenchanted youth—after a spate of sinful living—for personal worth and lasting love. Some are turning to the life-changing dynamic that revealed religion offers even the most profligate. (CT)

Teenagers by the droves ask whether life holds any real prospect for them or whether they belong to the apocalyptic generation. (NSF, 8)

Death

For all modern man's break with the supernatural and the eternal world, he seems unable to reconcile himself to any conviction that he is merely a temporal creature whose three-score years and ten are a prelude to mere nothingness. (NSF, 81)

We Americans bury our dead, as anthropologists are driven to comment, in a way that gives them a final semblance of being alive. That is not the only indication of our refusal to yield to the final reality of death. We are now reaching for a pseudo-immortality—maybe even a doubling of man's present life-span—through the continual replacement of human organs. Science is being looked upon as the giver of immortality in this body. (NSF, 82)

The philosophic case for immortality is not credible, and nobody believes that science will finally stave off human death. If all the options for immortality have expired, then every day simply brings us nearer the grave, and life diminishes daily in worth. (NSF, 75)

The complaint that a good God would afford the righteous uninterrupted happiness in this life is freighted with difficulties all its own. It is not only that its ideal of human existence is already fashioned by utilitarian standards—a maximum of pleasure and a minimum of pain—which would render it impossible to trace the outlines of divine purpose not only in the experiences of Job, but in the life of Jesus. If the divine norm for humanity—even perfect humanity—is pleasure only, if God is engaged in the promotion of a perpetual program of human comfort and delight in this life, then the record of human history is completely enigmatic. But if, as the Bible itself affirms, the divine intent is quite removed from such hedonism, and man's present life is to be evaluated not as a unit complete in itself, but rather as a preparation and discipline for eternity, in which the courageous bearing of pain and sorrow and the triumph over them by faith play a conspicuous role, then indeed the whole picture assumes a different perspective. Indeed, the Scriptures take sharp exception to the very notion of the *righteous*; man is a sinner, a creature in moral revolt against a holy God, and from whose hand the just penalty of death—of divine displeasure issuing in eternal separation from God and all things good—is man's only proper expectation, were it not for the grace of God. Where are the *righteous* who suffer, unless we mean only those who have not personally transgressed, or infants, and here the extent to which we may properly speak of suffering has its limitations. That a theodicy—the justification of the divine permission of natural and moral evil in the universe— demands some additional chapter to the experiences which this world affords for those who in repentance appropriate the divine mercy and its pledge of eternal bliss, is apparent indeed, but it is not *this life*, but the life to come, to which the whole biblical tradition looks for the complete vindication of the righteousness of God. Indeed, it is not the sufferings of men which constitute for the Scriptures a reflection on the justice of God, so much as His failure to assign to immediate condemnation the sinful human race. It is to the divine provision of atonement that the Bible points, as justifying both the postponement of punishment of the wicked and the acceptance of those who come to God by faith. (NDG, 36-37)

Lifestyle

As I see the lifestyle issue, a fundamental thing is the mindset and approachability of the Christian as a person. I don't think any staggering difference between "haves" and "have nots" is going to compensate for the lack of simple Christian gentility and approachableness. Lifestyle begins there—when a person is a person among persons. (RJ)

To an unregenerate world, not only will Jesus seem out of step with reality, but so will his disciples. Think and act like the world and the world will embrace us, for then being a Christian doesn't make a speck of difference. But truly live in the Spirit world as did early Christians and worldlings will consider us zombies—over the brink and stark mad. (CCDC, 51)

One sure way to frustrate evangelical awakening is for Christians to effusively give Sunday to God but, for the rest of the week, to accommodate a secular lifestyle shaped by craven greed. (CMSS, 21)

The Bible indicates that sin will continue until the final end of human history, and apostasy grow worse and worse, yet that is no reason for acquiescing in it and abandoning ourselves to it. (CH)

Help our generation find a new constellation of critical concern. The torch of morality and conscience, of love and compassion, of freedom and hope, needs to be refueled. Live by the mighty truth and power of God. Live above the sludge of our sick society. (CCDC, 143)

We are on the threshold of the decade of destiny, in the last generation before we leave behind the twentieth century, the end of one century and the beginning of another. What spiritual situation do we bequeath not only to those who follow us, but also to our contemporaries? (TGC, 43)

Man's character is ultimately defined by the character of his god. (GRA V, 9)

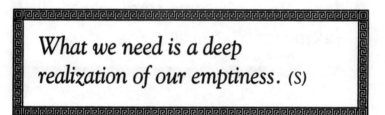

What we need is a deep realization of our emptiness. (S)

There is also the tendency to replace great church music by a barn-dance variety of semi-religious choruses; some churches have almost become spiritualized jukeboxes. (UCMF, 19)

MEDIA

Our tongue-polluted culture thrusts upon us endless soap operas and talk shows we could do without, a parade of automobiles, perfumes and record albums that we neither want nor need, and novel philosophies and moral aberrations that we ought to avoid and flee. Madison Avenue prospers on a genius for disguising the truth and distorting the word. (CMSS, 28)

Two powerful forces—in many ways the most fantastically potent influences known to the history of man—are today pursuing and competing for the beleaguered human spirit. On the one hand, the God of Judeo-Christian revelation, whose truth and Word nullified pagan deities in the ancient past, still holds modern secular man wholly answerable to the theistic exposition of human life. . . . On the other hand, the secularizing speech of audio-visual technology more and more sets the tone for human thought and conduct. . . . So astonishingly clever and successful have been these media in captivating the contemporary spirit—haunted as it is by moral vacillation and spiritual doubts—that Yahweh's ancient exhortation to beware of visual idols would seem doubly pertinent today. (GRA I, 17-18)

It should be obvious that if the truth of religion does not penetrate to the centers of communication, even as a live issue of debate, it must remain outside, where the inevitable penalty will be a posture of reaction on the margin of the modern world. (FAF, 176)

The emergence of the electronic church indicates that many people hunger for a personal faith. Much of this programming encourages an experiential religion, which, however, in the absence of adequate biblical teaching, can lead to theological error. (CT)

Television has helped inure us to the lustful look and casual sex, to prostitution and adultery, while it devalues evangelical morality as a vestigial remnant of the dinosaur age. (CMSS, 40)

Our society's main source of high culture is television, which replaces the cruelties of the Roman amphitheater by programmed violence and dignifies immorality with theatrical subtlety. The titillated masses eagerly scramble aboard this pre-routed cattle car that transports them free of charge to an intellectual Auschwitz. For a half-hour prime-time soap opera they exchange the hard-won moral heritage of the ages. (CH)

Contemporary fiction, television and the cinema become potent instrumentalities for a seductive revision of the established standards. Values that the Judeo-Christian heritage treasures (monogamous marriage, fidelity, chastity) are viewed as enslaving obstacles to self-fulfillment. This warped view of life empties into a disenchanting glory. (WT)

In Christian use the word "maturity" means quite the opposite of its connotation in current secular media. Networks designate the most offensive television programs—those deemed possibly harmful to children—as "for mature audiences only." Christianity measures maturity by a very different yardstick. (GRA IV, 504)

Books

The banality of television is driving more and more viewers to good reading. Books that confront the reigning ideas and ideals of an age are like earthquake tremors that signal impending disaster and prod people toward safer refuge. (WS)

I went to college primarily to get an education. I became interested in books, an expensive investment, but I have learned they are good friends. I have consciously sought out good scholars across lines, and frontier scholars within the evangelical community as well, for dialogue and exchange. (E2)

If we are to make a turning-impact, young evangelicals must become lovers of books and of truth; we need more tough-minded scholars to do battle with the intellectual philistines of our day as Augustine, Luther and Calvin did in theirs. (RB)

I think there will always be a place for the printed word. The printed word is somehow materialized and planted in history in a way in which the other media programs are not. Radio and television are under immediate program pressures that cancel viewer impressions, while printed material has a built-in possibility of permanence. (RJ)

The scholars who have influenced the course of theology in recent centuries have been men who not only thought and taught, but who wrote, and we live especially in an age when it is felt that one who has anything worthwhile to say will find his way into print. (FYPT, 94)

Art

Evangelical Christianity in its concentration on the moral aspects of goodness has tended to neglect the aesthetic; this is a misfortune, indeed, at a time when beauty and the arts and music are threatened by commercial, sensual and pornographic forces that impact even upon the church and its art forms. (GRA VI, 252)

The Bible does not say much about aesthetics (as we understand the term) and for good reason. But evangelicals have long said even less, and in the present cultural context they pay heavily for this neglect. In recent decades, however, there has been a developing evangelical interest in art and aesthetics, not without risk. (TGC, 122)

The modern focusing of beauty only in terms of visual gratification reflects the fragmented experience of a generation adrift from comprehensive meaning. There is nothing ethically neutral about the Old Testament conception of beauty. The Bible associates beauty with worship and divine purpose and righteousness. This is a far remove from the modern emphasis on "art for art's sake" and the complete subjectification of meaning in art and its isolation from the attestation of God's glory. (TGC, 123)

If one believes that God made human beings to think His thoughts after Him, one will not stock one's soul with salacious literature or steep his spirit in pornographic publications. (TGC, 120)

Journalism

Much newspaper and magazine space today is devoted to the deranged aspects of twentieth-century civilization. Perhaps this entered into the thinking of the wit who defined journalism, no doubt somewhat facetiously, as "the art of knowing where hell will break loose next and having a reporter on the spot." (SCP, 17)

In a day when newspapers and magazines were not yet, the gradually increasing books of the Bible were the divine bulletins to the human race. Running through all these accounts was a single editorial note, that Jehovah guides the affairs of individuals and shapes the destiny of nations. His staff of correspondents was second to none. Let any editor find a man to write the story of the early Hebrews more capably than the

leader and legislator Moses. Let any editor find a war corre-
spondent better equipped to tell the story of Israel's first expe-
ditionary force than Joshua. Let any editor find an essayist
more competent than Job. Let any editor find a columnist
more readable than Solomon the proverbialist. Let any editor
find a religious columnist more heart-searching than David
the psalmist. These are Jehovah's scribes, and the Bible is
Jehovah's newspaper. (SCP, 18-19)

Place at the head of the modern missions magazine the
Apostle Paul with his world-vision and zeal, for it is a man of
Paul's type that belongs there. (SCP, 19)

Had the modern press been in existence when the great
events of Bible history took place, of its own accord it would
have been interested. News stories and feature articles would
have centered about many personages and happenings familiar to the Bible student. Adam's biography, the first murder
story, the disappearance of Enoch, the strange prophet of the
Flood and his ark, Abraham's deliverance of Lot during the
invasion of Chedorlaomer and his confederate kings, the rise
of the prisoner Joseph to Egyptian rulership, the adoption of a
Hebrew child by the Egyptian queen, the disappearance of
the prince Moses, the slaying of the first-born, and the series
of ten plagues are but a few of the pre-Exodus accounts with
tremendous news value. (SCP, 20)

Instead of allowing the media to crowd out the Mediator,
the claim of the Mediator must be affirmed upon and through
the media. (CT)

The secular mentality scorns, satirizes, and caricatures the
"moral meanies." Secular press and media—skeptical as they
are about permanently good news—tend to lump the gospel
with the dinosaur age. For some of this misunderstanding
evangelicals have only themselves to blame. They have not
enthusiastically channeled dedicated young Christians into
the media and other public careers. (BPP)

Christians and Media

Evangelical educational institutions have used the media for fund-raising, but they have not by and large used the media to promulgate biblical world-life convictions. (TGC, 111)

Our evangelical colleges and seminaries ought to provide at least some training for a mass media age in which the world is fed up with words but is starved for the Word of life. (FAF, 192)

In our media-oriented age I would encourage every student who goes to college to take at least one course in journalism and in creative writing, even if one ends up able to do nothing more than post a letter to the editor! In that event at least the editorial page is not abandoned to radicals. But if one is going into a professional career, one ought to consider the great secular schools of journalism, for instance Medill, to learn the techniques and come to know others who across the years will be co-workers in the field. (RJ)

Today the religious journalist can fly over the ancient Bible lands in a matter of hours; in a few days he can cover the distances that once discomfited Moses and the prophets; and in just a few weeks he can retrace Paul's extensive missionary journeys. In a single day he can address more people than did Jesus of Nazareth in His total public ministry, and by a single effort on radio or television he can reach an audience larger than the entire population of Palestine and the Mediterranean area in the apostolic age of the church. (FAF, 159)

To neglect mass media and modern scientific aids for evangelizing the earth is a sin for which twentieth-century Christians might well be held specially responsible. Using these tools does not mean attempting to convert men by reliance on gimmicks and projects including Madison Avenue promotional techniques, for it is the Holy Spirit alone who gives new life. . . . There must be open recognition, however, that contemporary Christians dare not try to work and witness for God as if they still lived in "a pre-radio, pre-television, pre-electronic era." (EBC, 43-44)

We need an evangelical task force fully aware that a cadre of influential intellectuals—one that constitutes only 15 percent of the population of the United States—largely shapes the thinking of government, business, education, and the media. (CCDC, 133)

As Christians we need to turn our spirits to God's heavenly Talk-Show. . . . This Divine Speaker is waiting for people to converse with him, to spend unhurried time with him, the God of the Ages, the Eternal One who wants more than a three-minute long-distance call or a five-minute parking stop for a "hello" and "goodby." (CMSS, 28)

Christ is heaven's last Word. In his judgment of men and nations, all the pseudolords will grope for words. The media will belatedly hail the Mediator; Christ the Great Communicator will be prime time. (CMSS, 10)

Many Christians now live among neighbors who, swept by tides of immorality, fear herpes more than they fear Hades and some even think God is a lofty synonym for gobbledygook. (C)

MORALITY

Christian ethics derives its content and sanction and dynamic and goal from God—not from some inference from anthropology or sociology. It does not approach the problem of morals from the manward side and attempt to work its way to God. It is not only super-social and super-national, but supernatural. (CPE, 188)

The Bible nowhere views God's goodness as a supreme heavenly exemplification of, or divine conformity to, a perfection first discovered in man and the world and then projected upon divinity. Rather, it roots the conception of God's goodness in the living God's own self-revelation in the history of his people. (GRA VI, 251)

Christian ethics insists upon the unitary character of truth and the universal validity of moral norms. It is not ultimately defended by a hopeful appeal to non-rational considerations that are valid only for those who accept them and that admit no test besides existential commitment. (CPE, 145)

Neither the inception nor the demise of the Hebrew theocracy nullified an original divine creational morality that universally survived original sin and the fall of humanity. This creational ethic included the institution of monogamous marriage, of work as a legitimate human activity, and of structures of authority. It presumably commanded in principle whatever the Decalogue enforces. (TGC, 150)

The connection between biblical ethics and all speculative systems is fluid. . . . There is a shuttle service between the two, but even identical ethical propositions do not imply a precisely identical content. Sin and corruption in fallen human life frustrate the natural morality of man. . . . This distortion of moral content in man is so severe that the surviving content is no longer serviceable as the basis of a morality of special revelation. The ethics of Jesus Christ is no mere supplement or capstone for the ethics of Plato, Aristotle, Kant, Hegel, Royce, or Brightman. Any attempt to conceive of Christian ethics as a subspecies of speculative ethics does not account for two vital factors: special revelation and ethical revolt. (CPE, 146)

Moral imperatives, according to modern humanism, are mere culture prejudices; the Ten Commandments and the Sermon on the Mount are dismissed as fundamentalist fetishes. (CCDC, 143)

No society that disregards ethical finalities can long postpone ignominious collapse. (CMSS, 99)

The perverse notion that democracy is incompatible with moral absolutes spells for democracy inevitable collapse into chaos. The flipside implication of this notion is that only totalitarian powers deal in moral absolutes, a conclusion that credits tyrants with being monitors of the good. The fact is, of course, that by arbitrarily imposing universal rules tyrants simply reduce the good to bureaucratic preference. (CMSS, 19-20)

What distinguishes the present moral order in America from that of earlier generations? Simply this: Today's secular *mind*set rests as never before upon a nonbiblical *will*set. (CMSS, 19)

Fierce moral relativity is encompassing our secular society. Having lost its biblical moorings, our age stifles its conscience and displays an utterly shameless sensuality. One cannot but note the rampant perversion of sex, the breakdown of family life, the cruelty and inhumanity evident in the ready massacre of fetal life. One must mention also the failure of the great universities to sustain fixed moral values, the inability of humanism to mount ethical resources requiring self-sacrifice, and the widening effort by frontier scientists to gloss over the ethical and moral implications of their experiments by an appeal to mere utilitarianism. (CH)

Close the churches and synagogues and banish the Bible, prohibit public evangelism, staff the universities only with atheists (as totalitarian rulers would prefer) and the temper of our society would change swiftly. (WT)

Despite the crude charges about Christian conduct circulated at first by hostile Jews, opponents of Christianity stood with its friends in attesting to the purity of life it engendered, and to the "new world of moral power, of earnestness, and of holiness" in which believers moved. Pliny felt compelled to inform Trajan that his examinations, instead of finding anything criminal or vicious, disclosed the Christian gatherings to be concerned with self-confirmation in conscientious and virtuous living. (CPE, 437)

The vision of a new society is essentially biblical; the demands for social justice have their roots in the prophetic religion of the Bible. (NSF, 46)

The apostolic truth that the company of the redeemed constitutes a new society all too soon gave way to the larger ecclesiastical ambition to Christianize the outside world. (ACSE, 72)

A marked deterioration in American society, indeed in Western society generally, has arisen at the very time when evangelicals have been emerging from the subculture into the culture. (CMSS, 14)

Skepticism concerning commitment to God by those out-side the churches stems in part from the virtual obliteration of theistic claims from the public schoolroom, in part from the spiritual atrophy and intellectual softness of a generation preoccupied with material and secular concerns, and in part from uncritical tolerance of others' religious views that denies ultimate allegiance to any view. (GRA V, 15)

Human beings are prone to opt for the values they have inherited, that is, for tradition. Tradition can be adduced on many sides of an issue and mean many things; it can be invoked both to accredit and to discredit causes. Different countries have different cultural mixes. . . . An appeal to Christian tradition may be fully appropriate in the public arena . . . as long as it does not encourage a misimpression that tradition is self-justifying and does not dissolve the logos of law into the prevailing ethos. (CMSS, 116-17)

Others may seek to recover society from its moral collapse by calling for a relatively higher standard than prevails in the *Zeitgeist*. Christian ethics must protest that a culture raised only on such adjustments will soon again decay. It proclaims instead the changeless absolutes of revealed morality. Social relevance is written on its every word. (CPE, 219)

We must confront the world *now* with an ethics to make it tremble, and with a dynamic to give it hope. (UCMF, 60)

Fund-raising techniques and themes once viewed with dis-dain are becoming as common in evangelical circles as botanical hairdos and skin-grafted jeans in secular society. (TGC, 100)

Major controversial issues are whether Christian institu-tions should actively seek funding from nonevangelical foun-dations; whether familiar biblical passages on stewardship can properly be channeled into solicitations for modern parachurch movements; whether even evangelical enterprises may be guilty of "bait-and-switch" tactics; whether a "prosperity theology" is a legitimate means of enlisting donors; whether premium offers, including cheap trinkets depicted as having intrinsic spiritual power, are akin to medieval indulgences; whether so-called "junk mail" can in good conscience be represented as priority personal correspondence. (TGC, 100-101)

Seldom is the fund-seeker content to mention a need for which he is "looking to the Lord in faith" without the further suggestions that the Lord in turn is looking to the letter's recipient to handle the matter in His absence. (TGC, 102)

The error of the prosperity theme is not its emphasis that God blesses commercial integrity and sacrificial stewardship, nor that business success is attributable to divine providence, but rather its conversion of stewardship into a material prosperity tool, its attachment of giving to the expectation of personal financial benefit, its correlation of spirituality with material gain. (TGC, 104)

Few factors permanently motivate the giving of believers more than a clear, unambiguous definition of objectives enunciated by a leader perceived to be trustworthy. (TGC, 110)

As the cognitive center of the evangelical movement, the Christian campus must place promotion and funding conspicuously in the service of preserving, propagating and vindicating truth. (TGC, 111)

At one time Ethics might have been considered a dull hobby of a duller academician. This is not true today. Ethics is the incisive and universal requisite for survival. (CPE, 13)

The notion that an ethic of principle is inherently legalistic and impersonal rises from sheer misunderstanding. Any pattern of conduct may, of course, slip into formality and legalism simply because men easily shun the highest require-ments of moral decision. But to assert that observance of ethical principles necessarily is legalistic and depersonalizes the moral agent is an arbitrary claim. . . . The facts are the other way around. An unprincipled, and hence unpre-dictable, pattern of conduct necessarily violates personal rela-tionships, while an ethic that is truly promotive of personal concerns and predictably fulfills the requirements of love will not violate universally valid moral principles. (FAF, 138)

On many important contemporary issues we are left to make inferences from such biblically revealed principles as the dignity of human life, the corruption of human nature, the indispensable role of civil government. Shall we, for example, rely on nuclear energy even for peaceful purposes, rather than on more traditional alternatives, despite menac-ing reactor malfunction possibilities and waste disposal prob-lems? On such issues Christians have no more knowledge than do humanists or other non-Christians who weigh the probabilities for harm against the probabilities for good. To be sure, Christians will decide the matter not on the basis only of economic factors, or of selfish advantage to the pre-sent generation, but in view of the value of human life and of ecological concerns alongside constructive harnessing of the forces of nature. But one nonetheless makes the best decision he can in view of the available empirical data illuminated by biblical principles. (TGC, 142)

By freeing moral decision from the authority of divine commandments and objective moral principle, the new morality continually threatens to debase *agapē* into *eros*. (FAF, 142)

Not only is this a go-go generation unsure where it is going, but ours is also a go-go-going culture that scarcely sus-pects it is about gone. (NSF, 9)

NATURALISM

The conviction that nature is man's widest and deepest environment now dominates virtually the entire Western intellectual world. (GRA I, 13-14)

The first article in the modern confession of faith is, "I believe in nature almighty." Any world beyond nature is, by presupposition, relegated to the mythological category. Nature is the "maker of heaven and earth, of Jesus Christ, and of whatever gods there be," and is the maker of reason and morals too, simply because nature is ultimate. (RMM, 254)

The real alternatives to the discard of biblical theism were now seen to be not a restatement of classic idealism in modern dress, in which some elements of Christianity were retained, some rejected, and most of them transformed, but rather a thorough naturalism in which every trace of Christianity, insofar as possible, would be eliminated. The genuine option was not a non-Christian metaphysics blended with a sub-Christian ethics, but an inversion which went the entire distance. (DWT, 55)

Ours is the first generation in history to attempt to build a culture on naturalistic relativism. (CCDC, 35)

The modern mind reached its naturalistic terminus not at once but by a gradual process, because it needed first to emancipate itself from concepts which once were thought to belong properly to its perspective, but which more and more were seen to have been borrowed, by an overlooked debt, from the Hebrew-Christian view of things. (DWT, 38)

To declare that nature alone is the ultimate real, so that all reality takes its rise in and through differentiations of the natural world, is to declare at the same time that man is essentially an animal and that moral distinctions are only subjective and relative. It is to deny, that is, the reality of anything—gods, souls, values, or anything else—unsubject to time and change. (DWT, 41)

If impersonal processes comprise reality, naturalism has no consistent basis for identifying man as the evolutionary cap-stone, let alone for adducing universal and permanent human rights, or for championing the weak and impoverished rather than affirming the survival of the fittest. (TGC, 129)

What specially attracts liberal arts students to naturalism is its emergence in the form of humanism, a philosophic system that adds to the naturalistic agenda a program of social ethics. . . . This correlation of a humanist agenda of social ethics with a naturalistic world view has been attacked from right and left as a philosophical monstrosity that defies logical consistency. (CMSS, 87)

God is not an absentee sovereign but nature's everpresent ground and administrator: nature is no closed, self-sufficient activity. Standing perpetually in providential relationships to man and the world, God is no less implicated in the falling of the rain than in the resurrection of the Redeemer. (GRA VI, 15)

God has much more in mind and at stake in nature than a backdrop for man's comfort and convenience, or even a stage for the drama of human salvation. His purpose includes redemption of the cosmos that man has implicated in the fall. (GRA II, 99)

If the heavens declare only the prevalence of industrial smog, if day unto day uttereth only the chatter of the mass media, then the glory of God as veiled by technocratic scientism is conceivably indeed a form of judgment. (GRA II, 101)

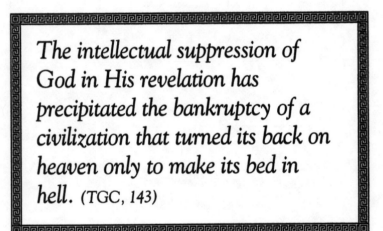

The intellectual suppression of God in His revelation has precipitated the bankruptcy of a civilization that turned its back on heaven only to make its bed in hell. (TGC, 143)

PHILOSOPHY

The whole frame of reference within which modern man seeks the meaning of life and the solution of his persistent problems displays its inadequacy in test after test. No era so replete with inner tension, so empty of synthesis, is found in the history of philosophy, except perhaps for the years 200-100 B.C. Every conceivable merger of propositions is consummated in the matrimonial mart of modern thought. (DWT, 12)

The striking reversals of modern philosophy have been necessitated by non-Christian answers to the cardinal problems of God, man and the universe. (RMM, 8)

Much philosophy now debunks even reason itself, and that can only be self-destructive. The great systems of conjectural philosophy are spent and obsolete; the entire development of modern philosophy stands at a crossroads of uncertainty. (WS)

For more than a century and a half modern philosophy has regrettably minimized the role of reason. Kant disjoined it from the spiritual world, Darwin naturalized and constricted it within the physical world. Dewey allowed it only a pragmatic or instrumental role. . . . A segment of evangelical Christianity nonetheless maintained its insistence upon the Logos as integral to the Godhead, the universe as a rational-purposive order, and man's finite reason as related to the image of God. (ERCT, 78)

163

Modern philosophy progressively stifled the biblical doctrine of divine transcendence and all but strangled it. First it obscured special revelation and detached transcendence from any significant doctrine of divine creation. The reality of the transcendent had already been weakened by the dilution of revealed theology into natural theology, for on the basis of natural theology God could be known only as an inference from the not-God, and not in terms of his own self-disclosure. (GRA VI, 38)

The prevailing philosophy today, whether it be the less deliberate, less self-conscious views of the lay mind or the professional and technical theories of the scholars, is the philosophy of humanism or naturalism. (RMM, 9)

Instead of eradicating religion, contemporary naturalism has in fact precipitated in the human heart a great spiritual vacuum and an ineradicable curiosity about transcendent reality that modern man fills with all sorts of cults and aberrations. The communist goal of extinguishing religion has failed even in rigidly controlled totalitarian societies like Russia and its satellite countries. (GRA IV, 583)

Deconstructionism

So-called deconstructionist philosophers, paced by Jacques Derrida, demand the dismantling of the entire Western tradition of philosophy and theology, with its emphasis on objectively existing Deity. . . . Derrida seeks to banish not only the "Greco-Christian God," but to strip away also any eternal and immutable Logos—any "logocentrism"—that permeates the universe. He seeks release from formal logic, and from the desire for verification, and projects an evolving fluid logos and open spectrum of verbal signification. The one sure result is a nihilistic assault on the Judeo-Christian heritage; no longer does the word "god" refer to a singularly unique metaphysical being. (TGC, 135-36)

We would misread the self-styled deconstructionist movement if we totally disdain its repudiation of Western metaphysical theology. In view of the almost endless succession of
new vogues in theology—the anthropological and post-
positivist versions of theology in recent modern thought, the
endless medieval theorizing about divine Being, the ready
Greco-Roman objectification of conflicting deities—have not
many of us believed also that for secular philosophy and theology wintertime was overdue? . . . The increasing entrapment of Deity in space-time processes, the ongoing religious
reductionism bent on compressing Deity until God gives up
the ghost, the attempt to derive a metaphysics from an analysis of finitude, are these not some of the many elements of a
metaphysical menagerie by which Western intellectual
thought has brought itself to an impasse? (TGC, 136-37)

In the deconstructionist movement, atheism no longer
entrenches itself as but one dissenting option among others,
but rather as the epistemic center of human experience, the
primal referent through which absolute emptiness replaces
absolute being. (TGC, 137)

The element of truth in deconstructionism, that the metaphysical and theological tradition of the West calls for radical
critique, is nullified by its intended dethronement of biblical
theism along with conjectural philosophy, and its deliberate
espousal of an atheistic alternative. Neo-paganism counters
the reality of the one God, counters confidence in divine creation, counters the gospel of divine redemption, counters the
singular incarnation of the Logos in Jesus Christ. (TGC, 137)

Modern Mind

The modern mind, unlike the Christian culture of the
Middle Ages, left no room for supernatural revelation and,
unlike the classic Greco-Roman mind, made no place for an
objective, eternal moral order to which man stands in unique
relation. (RMM, 22)

While the Hebrew-Christian view ranged itself formally on the side of the Greek idealistic case against naturalism, it stood opposed at the same time to the classic emphasis on the rational competence, in the realm of metaphysics, of the natural man in his state of sin; to the dualistic reduction of evil from a moral to a metaphysical problem; to the failure to identify the moral realm with the will of God; to the emptying of history of redemptive significance. (DWT, 27)

The relativistic outcome of modern philosophy has been knocking at the front door of contemporary man with loudening insistence. It has overtaken modern life not only in the area of sexual morality, but it has swept over entire segments of modern culture such as literature and the arts. It increasingly provides the conscious basis of contemporary man's outlook on life and existence. (GRA I, 42)

The modern mind is no longer clearly a mind, but a temperament, a mood subject to frequent changes. (GRA I, 41)

Modern philosophy has lost cohesion and is now largely given over to introspection. Secular philosophy almost always reads the twilight as a preface to the dawn rather than as a prelude to deepening night. (WS)

One must mention the emergence in the secular academic milieu of a competent vanguard of Christian philosophers, and this cadre of theistic academics is making its presence felt even on some of the nation's major campuses and is challenging the existential mood. (CH)

Names for God are indexes to philosophical approaches and systems, whether one thinks of Plato's *Idea of the Good*, Aristotle's *Prime Mover*, Plotinus's *One*, Spinoza's *Causa Sui*, Hegel's *Absolute*. (GRA II, 168)

PRESUPPOSITIONS

That God can be known, that divine revelation is rationally given and is to be rationally understood, is a basic presupposition of biblical theology. (GRA V, 381)

Christianity too has its basic "axioms" (the living God and intelligible divine revelation of truth) on which all its other claims depend. (CT)

No historian or scientist actually proceeds without presuppositions. Empiricists always operate on presuppositions which they cannot prove by their own methodology. Even evolutionary theory would collapse except for certain presuppositions that cannot be scientifically proved. . . . The scientific and historical approaches to meaning thrive on secretly negotiated lend-lease arrangements on which non-Christian scholars arbitrarily refuse to pay overdue interest rates and they ultimately deny any indebtedness to the theistic view. (GRA I, 231)

The idea of a presuppositionless observer is fictional; no observer is ever totally free of presuppositions. (GRA V, 25)

Whatever method of investigation is employed, we must of course abandon all claims to its absolute neutrality, since a presuppositionless methodology is an absurdity and, in fact, an impossibility. Every methodology has its presuppositions, and no interpreter is wholly—nor is he ideally so—free of presuppositions. No method is without underlying axioms and assumptions or aims and goals. Reliance on any given methodology involves a certain preunderstanding about the nature of the subject being investigated. The use of a method presupposes that the matter studied can be handled adequately by that method. (GRA IV, 388)

Because of the Fall, common axioms or common presuppositions, and hence common derivative principles, cannot be found between the theology of revelation and other religious systems or philosophies of religion. What men have in common is to be traced not through their systems of religious thought but through the *imago Dei*, which in some measure survives in every man. (GRA I, 405)

On the basis of the *imago Dei* that universally survives the Fall, even if blurred, the Christian can declare even of the nonbeliever that concerning certain moral emphases, "in your heart you know it's right." Even though natural law theory overstates its content in terms of a universally shared system of morality, some remnants of a creation-ethic survive in the conscience of every human being. (TGC, 33)

Nature is always viewed through one of several possible conceptual models. The African primitive reads it one way, the Western secularist another. Men of biblical outlook read it in still quite another. . . . Until just the last few centuries, not only Judeo-Christian theology but the main tradition of Western philosophy as well grounded the natural order in the supernatural and viewed nature as an intelligible context in which man and his purposes are meaningfully ensconced. (GRA II, 95)

If there is one ingredient in modern philosophy which made quite inevitable its removal from supernaturalistic to naturalistic terrain, it is the fact of its rejection of the principle of special divine revelation and the biblical miraculous. (DWT, 46)

That the world of nature is the prime reality, that the solution of all crucial problems will come by making the space-time universe, inclusive of man, the legitimate center of speculative interest, that it is the natural order above all with which a modern man must be familiar—what are these but characteristically modern notions, which came by the nineteenth and twentieth centuries to serve as the unexpressed ultimates presupposed in the educative centers of western culture, in western Europe and the British Isles and the United States before those, in turn, of Soviet Russia? (DWT, 42)

If man himself is ultimately the creator of all meanings and values—the meaning of the self and worth of society, the meaning of history and the worth of life, the meaning of the cosmos and the worth of truth—and even the meaning of meaning and the value of values—then a vast spectrum of myths, modern no less than ancient, are free to dominate the field of interpretation unchallenged. (GRA I, 163)

It makes a difference if we think ourselves to be merely self-seeking animals or fellow participants in a society answerable to divine justice, if we think nature is ours to manipulate or if we are responsible caretakers of the cosmos. (WT)

Secular man lives by a double standard—by the naturalistic credo which he affirms and reveres when it serves his purposes, and by hidden alternatives for action that he readily accepts whenever he prefers. (GRA I, 145)

The founding American fathers never declared or even intended that tolerance be an excuse or basis for dissolving all norms. Standing by itself, tolerance destroys even itself in destroying all norms. (CMSS, 19)

If divine revelation and not human reason is the source of truth, then man's mind cannot be viewed as inherently qualified to unravel all the enigmas of life. To say that man's mental powers are virtually divine contradicts both the basic

Christian axiom that God in his transcendent revelation is the only source of truth and its related emphasis, namely, that finite and fallen man even though gifted with the divine image is dependent upon revelation. When human reasoning is exalted as the source of truth then the content of truth is soon conformed to the prejudices of some influential thinker or school of scholars, or it may be conformed to the current consensus, sometimes dignified by the expression "the universal human consciousness." (GRA I, 226)

The modern critic who offers to deliver the biblical writer from supposed enslavement to an ancient culture about which we have little independent knowledge, all too often forces upon the writer a current culture prejudice that he, the critic, himself brings to the text. (GRA V, 408)

It is not, in fact, on conclusive historical evidence, but on inconclusive and frequently altered philosophical presuppositions that modern biblical criticism has tended to operate. (GRA IV, 81-82)

The Christian emphasis is that revelation supplies philosophy with its only secure presuppositions and that a coherent philosophy is the handmaid rather than the jealous rival of theology. (CPE, 149)

REVELATION

God reveals himself universally in nature, history, conscience, and the mind of man. But he reveals himself specially in Jesus Christ as attested by the Bible. (CT)

God reveals all that is necessary for us to know in order to serve him truly and obediently, and to share the blessings of redemption in this life and the next. (GRA V, 140)

Divine revelation palpitates with human surprise. Like a fiery bolt of lightning that unexpectedly zooms toward us and scores a direct hit, like an earthquake that suddenly shakes and engulfs us, it somersaults our private thoughts to abrupt awareness of ultimate destiny. By the unannounced intrusion of its omnipotent actuality, divine revelation lifts the present into the eternal and unmasks our pretenses of human omnicompetence. As if an invisible Concorde had burst the sound barrier overhead, it drives us to ponder whether the Other World has finally pinned us to the ground for a life-and-death response. Confronting us with a sense of cosmic arrest, it makes us ask whether the end of our world is at hand and propels us unasked before the Judge and Lord of the universe. Like some piercing air-raid siren it sends us scurrying from life's preoccupations and warns us that no escape remains if we neglect the only sure sanctuary. Even once-for-all revelation that has occurred in another time and place fills us with awe and wonder through its ongoing significance and bears the character almost of a fresh miracle. (GRA II, 17)

God stoops to state his purposes in our language and thought-forms which he first fashioned that we might think his thoughts after him, commune with him and serve him. (GRA V, 16)

In whatever mode God speaks, his divine revelation is a mental act, for it seeks to convey to the mind of man the truth about the Creator and Lord of life, and to write upon the spirit of man God's intelligible holy will. (GRA III, 271)

That God in his special revelation has spoken in sentences, that is, propositionally, is attested by prophets and apostles to whom special revelation came. The prophets are unqualifiedly positive that they speak messages from Yahweh. (GRA III, 481)

If divine revelation is cognitive and propositional, then God can reveal information about his immanent nature. Because of his intelligible revelation we can speak authentically about both his transcendent being and about his relations to man and the world. (GRA V, 102)

Revelation requires no dismemberment or boycotting of logic. Neither in part nor as a totality is the truth of revelation an illogical or nonlogical monstrosity. (GRA III, 303)

Christ and the prophetic-apostolic writers assumed the canons of rationality and expected men to exercise the logical laws requisite in meaningful thought. They did not authorize and introduce new and unheard of tests of truth, or some new and peculiar Christian technique of understanding. (GRA I, 232)

Meaning

Those who find a special "meaning" in theological statements can only do so by detaching such meaning from the patterns of logic and valid truth. Speech is used for a variety of purposes, but not for a variety of logics; there is one logic to which all propositions are answerable. Questions of truth and falsity are as relevant in theology as in mathematics and any other field. (GRA III, 385)

The Christian faith is a rational faith that rests on revelational fact and truth, a faith grounded in the self-disclosure of God in Christ as the ultimate reality and the ultimate reason. It calls therefore for reasonable reflection, reasonable decision, and reasonable service. (GRA I, 272)

Revelation finds its meaning for an evangelical in the truths about God and His relation to His creation which have been disclosed by special divine initiative and inscripturated. The Roman Catholic view of revelation . . . assigns equal value to the Bible and to church tradition, and concentrates revelation in the supposedly infallible interpretation of the teaching Church, especially the Pope. The more recent Neo-Supernaturalistic view, associated particularly with the name of Karl Barth and Emil Brunner, regards the Bible merely as a "witness" to revelation which presumably occurs continuously in a personal encounter with God conditioned upon human response, and denies the very possibility of doctrinal revelation. . . . Modernism, having sacrificed special revelation and miracle to the recent philosophy of science which insisted on the absolute uniformity of nature, absorbed special revelation to general revelation, regarded as simply another way of viewing the process of human insight from its upper side, and yet professed to salute Jesus Christ in His moral demands absolutely. Humanism, with its clear-cut denial of the reality of the supernatural, eliminated the ambiguity of the modernist's appeal to the so-called scientific method and recognized no legitimate function to be designated as revelation in distinction from human insight, subject to revision, gleaned through the application of the scientific method of sense observation and verification; here the concept of revelation, if admitted at all, is thoroughly secularized. (DWT, 132-33)

A faith in God which tries to establish its case on any proposition derived from general anthropology or philosophy of history or any other basis than the revelation of God in his Word is in no sense on the road to monotheism but is already on a one-way street to atheistic humanism. The Christian revelation of the living God propounds information about God on the basis of the Word of God, and not on what is professedly derived by analytico-synthetic examination of human experience. (GRA II, 123)

Naturalists emptied the idea of revelation of its former supernatural associations and deflated it into a vulgar common-place. Any report of scandal, the gossiping of a secret, tattling by a stool pigeon, even a private hunch about a winning horse in the fifth at Belmont was called a "revelation." (GRA II, 7)

That divine revelation never occurs in history and nature, that it is not validly intelligible but known only in inner decision and obedience—what are such premises but commitments grounded not in the Bible but in particular philosophical perspectives shaped by nineteenth- and twentieth-century religious theory? (GRA I, 191)

Neo-orthodoxy

The loss of revelation as a mental concept has had devastating consequences in modern theology. (GRA II, 12)

Neo-orthodoxy rejects any objective divine revelation of truths to chosen prophets and apostles and now objectively given in Scripture. (CT)

Neo-orthodoxy teaches that divine revelation is not propositional; it denies that God reveals truths about himself and his purposes. Small wonder that this God concept collapses into existential decision and finally death-of-God speculation. (CT)

The main agreements (of Barth and Brunner) are (*against classical liberalism*) first, that Christianity is not merely a higher expression of an essence shared in common with other religions but is essentially unique in view of a once-for-all revelation; second, that Christian experience is not intelligible in terms of categories derived from the psychology of experience outside the Hebrew-Christian tradition, in view of a supernatural work of regeneration by the Holy Spirit; third, Christianity involves a theology of special revelation (the Word) and at the center of this divine self-utterance is Jesus Christ; (*against orthodoxy*) first, divine revelation is not inscripturated in the sense of an infallible, trustworthy Bible in view of higher criticism; second, divine revelation is not conveyed in propositional doctrinal statements, but rather in terms of an "I-Thou" faith dialectic in which thesis and antithesis do not merge into a rational synthesis. (PD, 119, n. 143)

Neo-orthodoxy has no intention of reinstating a fixed and final theology. Indeed, it refuses even to concede that biblical theology is revealed. Doctrines, even prophetic and apostolic doctrines, are treated as devout theological reflection, not as revealed theology. (ERCT, 56)

The neo-orthodox notion that propositional truths or doctrines are in no sense divine revelation, but are merely pointers to revelation in the context of a nonintellective divine confrontation, totally contradicts what any reader of the Gospels can easily discover. (GRA III, 434)

Kerygmatic theologians as a whole insist that the text "points" to some invisible transcendent truth indefinable in logical categories and untranslatable into linguistic components. Many of us who have carefully observed these same texts over long periods and in many countries around the world must testify that never once in our lifetime have we come upon a single biblical passage in the act of "pointing." Indeed, the texts are said by a considerable company of modern scholars to point away from their obvious sense to so many hitherto veiled alternatives that even the profoundest contemporary critics seem wholly unable to agree on which of these lurking stowaways is friend or foe. (GRA III, 379)

The eye of the storm is currently shifting to two issues: the cultural conditioning of revelation, and the interpretation of Scripture. (CT)

If indeed all truth and meaning are culturally conditioned, no basis remains for selectively exempting certain preferred biblical specifics. If we elevate culture-conditioning into a formative principle, and insist that biblical theology falls within a culture-relative context, then the principle of relativity to culture applies not only to this or that isolated passage—whether about the seriousness of sexual sins or the role of women in the church; it extends also to the scriptural teaching that "in Christ there is nether male nor female" or that we are to love God with our whole being and our neighbors as ourselves, or that it is sinful to covet a neighbor's wife or possessions. It will not do to exhibit certain doctrines as the special strength of biblical religion if we simultaneously dismiss other teachings on the basis of pervasive cultural dependence. (GRA V, 404)

Natural Law

The marginality of revelation led to a secularizing of natural-law theory. In consequence, the validity of natural law was championed independently of any divine referent and solely on a foundation of human rationalistic determination. . . . Creative human personality becomes the source of law and rights. (TGC, 152-53)

The merit of natural-law theory lay in its insistence that positive law has a foundation deeper than the will of the sovereign or of the legislature, that a higher law is regulative of positive laws, and in its consequent exclusion of merely subjective, cultural, or evolutionary explanations of law. . . . Nonetheless the weakness of natural-law theory remained; without appeal to revelation, and simply by analysis of cosmic order or of human nature, it claimed to adduce a universally shared content of morality and law that critics could not really locate. (TGC, 153-54)

Medieval scholasticism "Christianized" natural law theory, which rests on the assumption that human reasoning, apart from divine disclosure, can identify a normative objective moral order. (TGC, 152)

Beyond its derailment of special revelation, what further distinguished medieval natural-law theory from the evangelical belief in a surviving creational ethic was its insistence that a universally shared body of law and ethics survives the Fall as a present possession of humankind. (TGC, 152)

The difficulty with natural-law theory is that moral philosophers who champion it do not agree among themselves as to the moral principles that it supposedly validates. No universally shared system of morality has, in fact, survived the fall of humanity. . . . Yet neither the lack of universally shared values nor the radical views of relativists requires a rejection of moral absolutes. (CMSS, 118)

It is indeed true that no universally shared system of truth or morality has survived since man's fall into sin. That does not mean, however, that no divine revelation of truth and the good therefore exists; indeed, despite man's rebellious will, God's universal revelation continually penetrates every human mind and conscience. Human beings may either declare all morality relative and thereby reinforce their condition of moral revolt or propose conjectural supports for shared ethical claims and thereby perpetuate the confusion of rival traditions. Or they may recognize God's revealed commands objectively published and exposited to a rebellious claim-torn world. (GRA V, 394)

Apart from recognition of the rational Creator of men made in his image and of the self-revealed Redeemer of a fallen humanity, who vouchsafes valid knowledge of the transempirical world, the modern Athenians are left to munch the husks of the religious vagabonds. (FMT, 155)

The recovery of interest in special divine revelation is one of the gracious providences of our century. It comes significantly at a time when the world must contend with the tactical initiatives of Communism and of irreligion. Protestant modernism succeeded in deflecting Western Christianity's theological interest from biblical revelation to natural theology. This renegade idealistic philosophy only briefly resisted a further decline to humanism. Evangelicals once reveled in the divine oracles; the modernists now asked whether God exists. Modernism's surrender of biblical revelation finally enmeshed American Christianity in the loss of the self-revealed God; in the non-communist world, as well as in the communist, naturalism surged to ascendancy. (ERCT, 64-65)

The Cosmic Christ goes before us, convincing a rebel creation that bears His marred image. The Great Apologist inscribes the case for theism ineradicably upon the souls of men. The Great Creator is astride His universe; daily He confronts and corrals every last man and woman with inescapable reminders of His power and deity and of judgment to come. (WCE)

Despite the knowledge explosion of our times few people today—churchgoers included—seem to know what God wills, what Scripture says, and what Jesus taught. (PED, 14)

When all the illegitimate halting-places are exhausted, the choice is between Nihilism and Revelationism. (PD, 40)

SCIENCE

The biblical view of God and the world did indeed con-
tribute in important ways to the rise of Western science; in
some respects modern science is therefore an extrapolation of
biblical theology. But influences other than Christianity are
far more responsible for the modern plundering and ravaging
of nature. The intellectual forfeiture of revealed religion and
the rejection by scientific naturalists of God and of created
man and nature facilitated the rise of modern technological
dominance. Not Hebrew thought, or Christian thought, or
the Protestant Reformers, are responsible for the post-
Renaissance view that nature is but an impersonal realm to be
manipulated, transformed or wasted to promote man's pleasure or profit. Only on highly nonbiblical assumptions
derived from an industrial view of nature could the earth be
regarded as literally "the cesspool of the universe," a dumping
ground not simply for sewage but for chemical pollutants and
atomic waste as well. (GRA VI, 263)

That the necessity for naturalism derives from modern science is, of course, an insincere claim; naturalism existed
before modern science, and modern science is compatible
with the full rejection of naturalism. Certain influential
philosophies of science are naturalistic, but that is very far
from saying that science requires naturalism; equally intricate
philosophies of science are idealistic. (DWT, 67)

No dogma more completely undermined the relevance of
the Hebrew-Christian tradition for the modern mind than

179

that of the absolute uniformity of nature, or law of universal causation, presupposed by experimental science. This principle precipitated the modern attack on miracle and came finally to mean that such overall Christian doctrines as creation of matter, of life, and of man, were extraneous to academic thought. (RMM, 79)

Throughout the history of modern science there have been warning voices, declaring that the assumption of nature's unconditional regularity has no unshakeable foundation, however much it was demanded as an experimental postulate. (RMM, 101)

Recent developments in philosophy and science have assailed this very insistence on the absolute uniformity of nature. The fetish of continuity, no less than that of inevitable progress and of man's essential goodness, is under attack by the most vigorous modern thinkers. . . . (RMM, 98)

Thus the startling insistences of recent science—especially Heisenberg's principle of indeterminacy and Planck's quantum physics—coupled with the anthropological failure to discover the missing links demanded by the continuity dogma, have combined to dispute the accepted view of nature. (RMM, 116)

The recent tendency to contrast scientific fact with religious myth is currently yielding, and remarkably so, to an age in which science now more candidly considers its own projections as tentative models and creative myths. Some of this change of perspective stems from the fact that earlier scientific dogmatisms have fallen upon hard times. Past claims to scientific finality frequently have had to be revised. There is no good reason to think that the claims presently in vogue are exempt from similar alteration or reversal. (GRA VI, 116)

Today the scientific world view stands charged with a grandiose remythologization of reality. (GRA I, 157)

Christianity says something powerful not only at emotional frontiers, but also and especially at the cognitive zenith of contemporary naturalism. It is quite willing to hear out "the other side," to allow the atheist and relativist to plead their cause, and to note how they strain to accommodate and even to promote certain imperatives as inviolable. It is the humanist in his unsteady humanism, the naturalist in his unjustifiable naturalism, whom we must engage. We must do so, moreover, not simply as crusaders for evangelistic decision, appropriate as that may be in its time and place, but in confrontation of both mindset and willset. We must dispute the axioms of neo-pagan thought, unmask a disposition under no absolute constraint to oppose eternal truth and a fixed good, and exhibit the self-legislated limits within which scientific empiricism lays claim to all truth and reality. (TGC, 140-41)

An advantage that science is often said to hold over theology is that it deals with empirically observable realities whereas theology is preoccupied with nonempirical metaphysics. The force of this representation depends obviously on a covert assumption that, because they are not empirically observable or verifiable, metaphysical realities are less significant or less real. But might one not with equal force insist that theology has over the physical sciences the advantage of dealing with invisible spiritual realities? (GRA I, 172)

The scientist has on the basis of empirical methodology no legitimate metaphysics at all. Electrons in distinction from centaurs permit deductions which seem at present to sustain rather than to refute them, but whether natural selection and electrons are less imaginative than centaurs may well depend upon which generation of scientists one asks. (GRA I, 173)

Science—in the modern sense of phenomenal knowledge gained by sensual means, requiring laboratory verification and subject to constant revision—is impotent to decide the issue of the reality or unreality of the supernatural. (DWT, 68)

To think of life as a lottery and of human survival as a gamble inevitably dissolves the assurance that "God works all things together for good to them that love him." . . . The man whose only security is in radar warning systems obviously knows nothing of the Christian's confidence that "none can pluck" him "out of Christ's hand." (GWSH, 10)

Social Concerns

To do nothing about social wrongs is to do the wrong thing. Simply to avoid civil disobedience is one way of needlessly giving carte blanche to radical causes. (PED, 106)

Christian duty requires courageous participation at the frontiers of public concern—education, mass media, politics, law, literature and the arts, labor and economics, and the whole realm of cultural pursuits. (TGC, 44)

God has a special eye for the poor, a special duty for the rich amid the seductive temptations that face both: the former, lust for things as the essence of life; the latter, love of riches. Christians are to stand on the side of the poor against exploitation, injustice and oppression; sensitive to human needs, they are to respond generously as God has enabled them. They are to do all this, moreover, not in a corner, but openly in the midst of mankind—not for ostentatious show, but to manifest what it means to be God's people. (GRA IV, 496)

The rise of the Euroamerican middle class is a remarkable exception in history, not a norm, and it imposes special stewardship opportunities and responsibilities upon Western Christians, especially in respect to the world missionary enterprise and humanitarian needs. (CH)

Response to the plight of the destitute is a prime test of social sensitivity. (CMSS, 104)

In the matter of expounding the biblical principles of social justice, of exposing unsound theories to open shame, of openly challenging race discrimination and civil rights compromises, the evangelical churches ought to have been in the *vanguard*. (ACSE, 123)

Why must the Church wait until the Supreme Court defines the issues (as in race relations) or until the Church is put in the position of merely reacting to somebody else's initiative? (PED, 16)

The Bible calls for personal holiness and for sweeping societal changes; it refuses to substitute private religion for social responsibility or social engagement for personal commitment to God. (PED, 107)

The temptation to stress evangelism only as "the Christian answer" and to withdraw from social confrontation is dangerous and one that Protestant orthodoxy had best avoid. (PED, 43)

Jesus of Nazareth cannot really be adduced as a precedent for that evangelical theological individualism which simply permits society to take its own course but offers no public protest against exploitation and dehumanization. (GRA III, 124)

The record of fundamentalist withdrawal from social concerns and preoccupation with personal evangelism has compounded an impression of public irrelevance. While evangelicals avoid internalizing religion completely, they have not in the present century escaped largely privatizing it. By making individual renewal the dominant concern, they lessen interest in the messiahship of Jesus among those who stress that the prophetic vision of Messiah embraces universal justice and peace as irreducible concerns of the righteous community. (GRA III, 122)

The troubled conscience of the modern liberal, growing out of his superficial optimism, is a deep thing in modern times. But so is the uneasy conscience of the modern Fundamentalist, that no voice is speaking today as Paul would, either at the United Nations sessions, or at labor-management disputes, or in strategic university classrooms whether in Japan or Germany or America. (UCMF, 34)

It was the failure of Fundamentalism to work out a positive message within its own framework, and its tendency instead to take further refuge in a despairing view of world history, that cut off the pertinence of evangelicalism to the modern global crisis. (UCMF, 32)

Why did evangelical Christianity concentrate its energies mainly in repudiating the non-evangelical deviations instead of expounding social ethics on Scriptural presuppositions? (PED, 27)

In the present explosive era of history the problem of acting on an acceptable methodology is an urgent one for evangelicals. It is one thing to deplore ministerial marches and picket lines and well-publicized public pressures; but if evangelical conscience is to be a remedial and transforming social force, then evangelical convictions require articulate mobilization on their own account. (GWSH, 60)

American Protestant orthodoxy has produced no unified social ethics or program of evangelical social action. Too long have evangelicals acted as if protest were proper only when directed against the liberals and their mistakes. It is high time the minority reached its majority and maturity. (PED, 22-23)

Today Protestant Fundamentalism, although heir-apparent to the supernaturalist gospel of the biblical and Reformation minds, is a stranger, in its predominant spirit, to the vigorous social interest of its ideological forebears. Modern

Fundamentalism does not explicitly sketch the social implications of its message for the non-Christian world; it does not challenge the injustices of the totalitarianisms, the secularisms of modern education, the evils of racial hatred, the wrongs of current labor-management relations, the inadequate bases of international dealings. It has ceased to challenge Caesar and Rome, as though in futile resignation and submission to the triumphant Renaissance mood. The apostolic Gospel stands divorced from a passion to right the world. The Christian social imperative is today in the hands of those who understand it in sub-Christian terms. (UCMF, 45)

While it is not the Christian's task to correct social, moral and political conditions as his primary effort apart from a redemptive setting, simply because of his opposition to evils he ought to lend his endorsement to remedial efforts in any context not specifically anti-redemptive. . . . Such cooperation, coupled with the Gospel emphasis, might provide the needed pattern of action for condemning aggressive warfare in concert with the United Nations Organization, while at the same time disputing the frame of reference by which the attempt is made to outlaw such warfare; for condemning racial hatred and intolerance, while at the same time protesting the superficial view of man which overlooked the need of individual regeneration; for condemning the liquor traffic, while insisting that it is impossible for legislation actually to correct the heart of man; for seeking justice for both labor and management in business and industrial problems, while protesting the fallacy that man's deepest need is economic. (UCMF, 87)

In our century, as I see it, Protestant forces seeking a better social order in America have mostly neglected the method of evangelism and the dynamic of supernatural regeneration and sanctification. (ACSE, 16)

Now it is true that the Church has a legitimate and necessary stake in education and legislation as a means of *preserving* what is worth preserving in the present social order, but it must rely on spiritual regeneration for the *transformation* of society. (ACSE, 16)

If the Church fails to apply the central truths of the Christian religion to social problems correctly, someone else will do so incorrectly. (ACSE, 82)

The twentieth century has cherished high hopes for socio-politico-economic reconstruction. First it trusted mass education to propound a new vision of society, then domestic legislation and possibly even international jurisprudence, and more recently it has looked to mob pressures and revolutionary techniques to bring about rapid social fulfillment. (ACSE, 9)

A great deal that passes for Christian social ethics today overlooks the primary responsibility of Christians to care for those within the body, simply because we have little sense of body within Christian circles any longer. (S)

Like third-world guerrillas, we often spray random machine-gun bullets at the status quo and in so doing sometimes accidentally (and sometimes not so accidentally) hit each other. Perhaps we are not always sure who our friends are, and worse yet, not really sure who the enemy is. (CCDC, 138)

Too often has the conscience of the church despite this holy vision become sluggish over the *status quo*, so that Christians imply to the world that things must remain as they are. (PED, 105)

When institutional Christianity yields to identification with reactionary rather than regenerative forces it secretly contracts its own suicide. (PED, 106)

The realm of evangelical expertise in social morality should be to identity why a situation is wrong, when and why it demands public confrontation, and precisely what the right alternative is. (PED, 18)

Evangelicals must learn to set the issues and even to initiate protest when lesser alternatives have failed and intolerable grievances persist. (PED, 21)

We need an evangelical coalition, one neither dominated nor exploited by existing agencies, to forge a broad consensus over against the major social evils of our time. (CMSS, 22)

If evangelical leaders could meet and draw up an agenda of priorities and concentrate on their commonalities rather than their differences they could forge an influential consensus within our society. (RB)

I'm gratified that evangelicals are finding their way back into the public arena, but disconcerted lest they act unwisely and lose their opportunity. (CT)

One need only know the history of the East or travel in most lands outside the Western hemisphere to learn how much of the modern response to human affliction has its roots in Christian compassion and motivation. Today in some countries humanistic or totalitarian agencies have largely taken over the administration of education, hospitals, and welfare programs generally; nonetheless the indebtedness of the world at large to the biblical view of God and man for such concerns is too ineradicably a fact of history to be ignored. (PED, 113)

The day will soon come when even those clergy who thought it better to be social activists than theologians will concede that social change motivated by bromide ideology leads to swift disenchantment. (WS2)

Governments are often kept from prompt involvement because of diplomatic, geographic or other deterrents; at any and every post and outpost the local church can easily become Good Samaritan on-the-spot. (PED, 114)

It is one thing to run away from sin; it is yet another to run up a flag for faith. (TGC, 42)

The social struggle cannot be won by bumper stickers. (PED, 15)

We must not be held at bay by the powers of this world, or defanged by the spirit of our age. We dare not grant the finality of the present world-establishment, or to seek only minor modifications of it. Give that world-spirit your little finger and your body and soul will soon also go with it. (TGC, 55)

Various Issues

[S]ociety is elaborating its own version of the "good life," one that deliberately incorporates much that has long been "off limits" for human dignity and decency. (NSF, 58)

What is underway is a redefinition of the good life, a redefinition that not only perverts the word "good" but perverts the term "life" as well. What is "good" is corrupted into whatever gratifies one's personal desires, whatever promotes self-interest even at the expense of the dignity and worth of others. In that fantasy-world of sinful desires, shameful lusts, and a depraved mind, sexual libertinism is good, coveting and stealing are good, violence and terrorism are good. (TGC, 40)

Modernity deliberately experiences this new immorality as an option superior to the inherited Judeo-Christian alternative. What underlies the atheistic commitment to novel sexual and marital and political patterns is a stultification of biblical conscience, an irreligious redefinition of the good, a profane willset. (TGC, 27)

It says something about our age that many of its intellectuals, including some theologians, are more concerned about eliminating supposed aberrations in sexual God-language in the name of feminine libertarianism than about stemming sexual aberrations and licentiousness in human relationships in the name of a holy God. (GRA V, 164)

The evangelical wing sees more clearly than the non-evangelical wing that homosexuality from the standpoint of the Bible is a sin, and ought not to be dismissed as a sickness. . . . They tend not to see the problem of civil rights, rights before the law. Non-evangelical churches see only the civil rights . . . and lose the biblical judgment of wickedness and the possibility of redemption. (VP)

The debate over the human or civil rights of homosexuals should not be confused by analogies with race discrimination or concerns of religious freedom; people are born black or white or brown but they are not born gay. Gays can and ought to alter their lifestyle even if we must not infringe upon their political rights. (CMSS, 103-4)

The worst affliction of the modern age is not AIDS, epidemic as it may be; atheism is, for it makes spiritual death unavoidable in this life and the next. For all that, AIDS is a plague that has arisen in a particular pagan era; its almost universal menace is a concomitant of a certain view of human life and its priorities. (TGC, 142)

The deliberate medical extinction of a million human fetuses a year exceeds the appalling evil of infanticide in pre-Christian paganism and approves a practice that civilizational conscience in all earlier decades considered reprehensible and morally vicious. It is supremely ironic that a society that declares human rights an absolute priority should retract the right to life of the fetal life it engenders. (CMSS, 103)

When childbirth would endanger the mother's life abortion can be morally justifiable. The fetus seems less than human, moreover, in cases of extreme deformity in which rational and moral capacities integral to the *imago Dei* are clearly lacking. The scriptural correlation of sexual intercourse with marriage and the family, furthermore implies an ethical basis for voluntary abortion in cases of incest and rape. (CMSS, 103)

I sometimes wonder what counsel would have been given to Joseph and Mary by activist churchmen informed of Mary's psychic visions, and their insistence that Joseph was not the father of Mary's expected babe. It is not too radical to predict that a clergyman insensitive to biblical realities and holding modern permissive views of sex might raise the subject of abortion and name a referral service. (CCDC, 58)

Nuclear power is no more evil than is matter (as some Greek philosophers thought); it is the use to which it is put that is decisive. (L)

The truth is that material priorities have emptied rather than filled the lives of the affluent. (GRA V, 15)

Inflation is a moral issue. A sound dollar is one of the best ways to help the unemployed, the poor, the elderly, the working class, and the nation as a whole. (L)

The United States should in the present world condition be second to no power militarily. But massive military budgets place an immense burden on modern nations; they continually damage themselves and provoke each other by this endless escalation. A bilateral halt in the arms race involving on-site verification should be an international objective. (L)

Christians must maintain a strong and sustained witness to Christ, the prince of peace and King of kings; must pray urgently for peace among the nations; must press upon these powers an awareness of the damage done by the arms race to each other and to themselves; and must deplore the self-condemning track record of predator powers whose expansionist policies provoke ever-escalating expenditures that might ideally be deployed to more constructive social uses. (CMSS, 106)

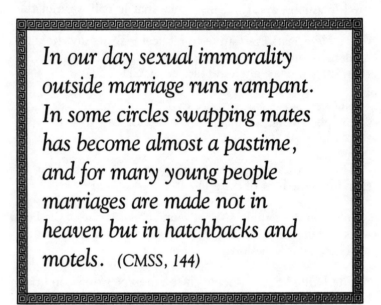

In our day sexual immorality outside marriage runs rampant. In some circles swapping mates has become almost a pastime, and for many young people marriages are made not in heaven but in hatchbacks and motels. (CMSS, 144)

SOCIALISM

The Marxist movement envisions the new man as intolerant of the status quo, hateful of the capitalist system, devoted whole soul to politico-economic revolution, disdainful of belief in the supernatural as a hurtful myth, and committed to dialectical materialism and state absolutism as the keys to future utopia. (GRA IV, 522)

The basic problem of modern society, as the secular revolutionaries see it, is that of economic inequality. The heart of their "gospel" is that Christ died for the redistribution of wealth, and that these infinite material resources are now to be universally resurrected by secular ecumenism. (PED, 41)

The "poor" existed long before capitalist economics, which is often blamed for their existence, and Marxism has not eliminated an impoverished class. (CCDC, 34)

The evangelical movement is woefully confused on free enterprise issues. While it staunchly opposes communism as an ideology of totalitarian atheism and statist restriction on human rights, especially religious freedom, it is ambivalent about Marxist economic analysis. Neither evangelical colleges nor seminaries prepare logic-wary young people for clear distinctions. Few seem aware that socialism is demonstrably a miserable failure in country after country where it has been tried, while Third World capitalistic countries like Korea and Taiwan have experienced economic revival. (COT, 399)

I think there are strengths to capitalism. But our failure to criticize capitalism in its operation—the shoddy record of production of obsolescence, the reckless depletion of natural resources, the prizing of profit over sensitivity to workers' needs, the bribery by multinational corporations, the big stake in smoking and cigarette production, despite the fact that we know it to be harmful, the alcohol traffic—gave a one-way street to the Marxists to criticize capitalism in such a way that our younger generation became enchanted with Marxism as an alternative. (S)

The constant prolongation of Marxist promises and the continual postponement of the anticipated utopias contradict socialism's own expectations. (GRA IV, 571)

Many evangelical schools failed to vindicate the values of capitalism and also failed to criticize its sins; thus they created an undeserved sympathy for socialism which consequently appeared benevolent. Many victims of socialism today would like to escape to capitalist countries. (CH)

Some Christian churchmen early in this century fell over each other in their rush to declare Jesus a socialist; some naively repeat the error today. (CH)

Evangelical Christians often speak of Christianity as a "revolutionary religion" and of the Nazarene as "the revolutionary Jesus." What they intend to emphasize thereby, however, is that the Christian challenge to the existing orders of society is thorough-going and radical—more so than that posed by an ideological alternative. But this way of speaking now has definite risks of misunderstanding, because of today's predominantly communist connection of the term "revolution." Moreover, not only communists but also some ecumenical churchmen exploit the idea of "the revolutionary Christ" and of Christianity as a "revolutionary" religion in order to confer ecclesiastical sanction upon Marxist economic ideas. (EBC, 59)

Socialism has failed woefully to live up to its promises, and communism even more so; the notion that they are benevolent is ill-founded. (CT)

Instead of the perilous propaganda that God is today speaking in revolution, both church and world need to hear what God has been urgently saying for centuries and is saying still, namely, that refusal to heed his commandments and to hear the gospel of Christ is what really underlies the plight of the modern world and the ailing condition of the church. (PED, 104)

SPIRIT WORLD

In the Bible God is the Supernatural, while all heavenly spirits, whether fallen or unfallen, belong to the created world. (GRA VI, 21)

When Scripture speaks of the heavenly expanses it does so not in terms of purposeless fireballs, dead stars, burnt craters, moon rocks and planetary rings; it suggests rather that personal beings populate the universe, beings who are continually oriented to the plan and purpose of the Creator. (GRA VI, 229)

The task of angels is essentially a ministry in the service of God; they perform what God decrees, and they are extensively engaged in worship of him. (GRA VI, 233)

While angels have a vital ministry in relation to man, they are not mediators between God and man. To worship angels is strictly forbidden since such worship would make them false gods. (GRA VI, 234)

The doctrine of angelology fell into disinterest in the twentieth century because of scientific preoccupations. With its empirical and naturalistic orientation and its explanation of external reality by impersonal processes, Western thought eroded faith in any invisible spiritual world. (GRA VI, 230)

Christian theology considers the modern repudiation of Satan as an aspect of man's spiritual revolt. (GRA VI, 230)

Modern philosophers and theologians are not alone in failing to take Satan seriously; it was Adam in Eden also, and we his descendants are dupes in the same tradition. (GRA VI, 239)

Capable of manifesting himself in many ways, including that of an angel of light, Satan appears in the Genesis account as tempter of the first human pair. (GRA VI, 237)

The New Testament doctrine of the good life can no more be elaborated without decisive reference to the Holy Spirit than can its doctrine of sin and evil without reference to Satan. (CPE, 441)

Pride and envy are usually said to have precipitated Satan's fall. (GRA VI, 236)

To the astonishment of our secular age, spiritism, demonism and even Satan worship have revived in recent decades as a phenomenon of civilized society. (GRA VI, 229)

The apostle Paul, that great theologian-evangelist-social critic, reminds generation after generation that we contend against powers that require supernatural rebuttal, and without the Divine Superpower and our own comprehension of who the enemy truly is, all our efforts will be in vain. (CT2)

THEOLOGY

Everyone has a theology. It may be a very shoddy one, and if it is shoddy, it will rise to haunt one in a crisis of life. It's my conviction that only a theology which has the living God at its center and that is rooted in Christ, the crucified and risen Redeemer, has the intellectual struts to engage the modern secular views effectively. (WR)

There was a time earlier in the Christian era when the evangelist's best ally was the theologian, whose forceful statements of the Christian revelation served to clarify the urgency of the task. But today many theologians themselves need to be evangelized. (FAF, 47)

We theologians become a self-endangered species when we leash our message to ghettos of faith and do not unleash it into the world for which it was intended. (TGC, 54)

The notion that the world could be saved from injustice and restored to righteousness by education, legislation, and socialization was the great error of modernist theology. The equally unsound notion that it can attain messianic justice through violence is the mistake of the theology of revolution. (BPP)

As Protestant liberalism dissolved confidence in the distinctive supernaturalism of Christian redemption, emphasis shifted to those latent forces which Christianity was said to share with other religions and which co-operatively could transform the social order. (ACSE, 111)

While Liberalism declared that the Christian scheme is "higher" than that of the world religions generally, it was forbidden to Liberalism—in view of its basic dogma of "continuity"—to declare that Christianity, in whole or in part, is different "in kind," is qualitatively unique in contrast with the other religions. Liberalism has not always made clear that this assertion that Christianity is "higher" was intended as a denial that it is qualitatively different. The proponents of Liberalism stressed that Christianity is so vastly superior to the other religions that the difference in degree "practically" comes to a difference in kind. They stressed that the psychology of Christian experience had something over and above to offer the psychology of Mohammedan or Buddhist experience. They emphasized the "relative absoluteness" of Christ and affirmed their personal faith that no higher incarnation of the divine than that in him would ever appear. They asserted the Scriptures to be different precisely because of the historical record which they afford of the beginnings of this distinctive movement. But all of this came in the end to a circuitous, and sometimes in the case of the so-called "heresy" trials, a very convenient, way of denying that Christianity is the only true religion, of denying that men without Christian rebirth could not see the kingdom of heaven, of denying that Christ Jesus is the only name under heaven given among men whereby they must be saved, of denying that the Bible is in an exclusive sense the Word of God written. That is to say, Liberalism's praises of Christianity and its content came in the course of repudiating what Christianity historically has asserted about itself. (DWT, 148-49)

To date, the ecumenical development has been more hospitable to theological openness and inclusivism than to definitive dogmatics. (FMT, 91)

For the third time in our century Continental Protestantism has tumbled into a morass of theological confusion and transition. Apprehension shadows almost all phases of current theological inquiry and reflection; what the final direction of the dogmatic drift will be is now wholly uncertain. (FMT, 9)

The most obvious defect of contemporary theological faddism is its mislocation of the problem of modern man. Whether modern man's special difficulty is specified as the use of religious language in a secular age, or as self-understanding, or as the supposed requirements of a scientific outlook, it is always falsely implied that no view of Christianity is possible for modern man other than one screened through empirical categories. (FMT, 151)

Protestant Christianity no longer responds to any one final authority. The sad result of its theological defection from the biblical norm shows in the chaotic condition of Continental religious thought. (FMT, 98)

One can more readily forgive empirical science and conjectural philosophy for seeking to correlate reason only with changing phenomena and animalistic development than one can excuse recent Christian theology for dissociating reason from the Divine Logos, from the image of god in man, from rational divine revelation, from a scripturally given truth of God. (WS2)

Either man himself projects upon the world and its history a supernatural reality and activity that disallows objectively valid cognitive statements on the basis of divine disclosure, or a transcendent divine reality through intelligible revelation establishes the fact that God is actually at work in the sphere of nature and human affairs. (GRA I, 45)

In a campus atmosphere of many viewpoints, students easily become skeptical of theological truth as something beyond their reach; instead, considerations of professional status and ecumenical eligibility bulk large. (FMT, 112)

Protestant participation in the dialogue with Rome is driven forward not so much by confident theological consensus and conviction as by an exasperating lack of such concurrence, and by the secret and perhaps strange hope that larger ecumenical conversations will shape a new unity in which Protestant consciousness can survive unhindered. (FMT, 98)

The strength of evangelical theism lies in its offer of religious realities that human unregeneracy desperately needs and cannot otherwise provide. In a time of spiritual rootlessness Christianity proclaims God the self-revealed heavenly Redeemer. In a time of intellectual skepticism, it adduces fixed truths about God's holy purpose for man and the world. In a time of ethical permissiveness, it offers moral absolutes and specific divine imperatives. In a time of frightful fear of the future, it presents a sure and final hope. In a time when daily life has turned bitter and sour for multitudes of humans, it offers a life-transforming dynamic. (COT, 389)

TRUTH

Truth is Christianity's most enduring asset. When all other things—the picketing and the protesting—pass away, it is the question of the truth of Christianity that will ultimately determine its endurance. (CT2)

That God is truth; that all truth is of God; that truth is for man's obedient understanding of his Creator, for the enrichment of man's own life, and for the greater good and service of mankind—these emphases are integral to the Christian view. (GWSH, 114)

Divine revelation is the source of all truth, the truth of Christianity included; reason is the instrument for recognizing it; Scripture is its verifying principle; logical consistency is a negative test for truth and coherence a subordinate test. The task of Christian theology is to exhibit the content of biblical revelation as an orderly whole. (GRA I, 215)

Never has the question been more important whether our beliefs are simply scientific tentatives, speculative conjecture, private psychic certitudes, or universally valid truth. (WT)

The truth of God does not collapse man's intellectual horizons, nor does it minimize the role of rational consciousness and cerebral cognition, nor forego rational coherence in viewing life and the world. (GRA I, 121)

The fundamental issue remains the issue of truth, the truth of theological assertions. No work on theology will be worth its weight if that fundamental issue is obscured. (GRA I, 14)

Neo-Protestant theologians have emphasized trust more than truth; minimizing the intellectual context and content of Christian decision, they have devalued the logic of Christian commitment. (PED, 74-75)

It is not surprising that in our generation theology has conferred Christian respectability on the category of myth. Although all five New Testament uses of the term myth are derogatory, myth is inoffensive to the theologian who dismisses the ultimacy of rational truth. (GRA V, 374)

The term *myth* has acquired a bewildering ambiguity of connotation in respect to religious thought. It has, in fact, become a "tramp" word. . . . To introduce the concept of myth in no way relieves us of the burden of asking what beliefs are literally true . . . and on what cognitive basis we affirm this to be the case. Contemporary neo-Protestant writers seem to employ the term myth as a linguistic device for evading the problem of truth. (GRA I, 68)

What Christianity taught the world of ancient thought, namely, that all truth is identical with the living mind of God, is forfeited in an age that assigns God and mystery to one realm, and man and rationality to another. (GRA V, 358)

The unlettered evangelist who urges his audience simply to "take the plunge" has found a twentieth-century counterpart in the theologian who exhorts divinity students to pole-vault into paradox. The costly consequence of this theology is that it neglects the very propositions that must be true if Christianity is to be true, and if faith is to be Christian. (GRA III, 487)

Beleaguered by indelicacy and indecency, by tastelessness and vulgarity, our sophisticated society is given on the one hand to a hatred of ultimate truth and on the other to irrational passion. There is little remembrance of a long-gone age when the calm reflection of a reasoned existence prevailed. (CMSS, 48)

The radical secularists dismiss fixed truth and unchanging values; they consider truth and morality culture-relative and man an autonomous animal. Yet they curiously champion social justice, and the universal and permanent dignity of man and his individual worth, ecological responsibility, and much else. Such moral mandates cannot be consistently derived from the naturalistic creed. These ethical imperatives reflect the fact that, for all his naturalistic stance intellectually, modern man is linked still, even if in a broken way, to the divine image in man and to God in his revelation. He adjusts his day-to-day life to a higher sphere than statistical averages superimposed on a planet supposedly born of an explosion. (WS3)

It is imperative to demonstrate as well as declare the gospel-truth. A hallmark of biblical Christianity is its irreducible distinction between a dead orthodoxy consisting only in words and a living, breathing faith. (PED, 83)

The apostles knew that the truth of truth, the truth of God, and the truth of the gospel stand or fall together. (PED, 77)

Truth-famine is the ultimate and worst of all famines. Unless modern culture recovers the truth of truth and the truth of God, civilization is doomed to oblivion and the spirit of man to nihilism. (PED, 75)

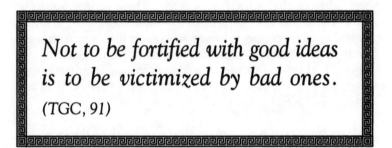

Not to be fortified with good ideas is to be victimized by bad ones.
(TGC, 91)

WORK

To use hammer, plane, chisel and saw belongs to a tradition which the Son of God himself reverences. When he used the plumbline, the God-man lost none of his glory. (ACSE, 52)

Man as a worker finds his archetype in God the mighty Worker. . . . Think of what was "all in a day's work" for the Almighty One! We read of his labor on the "First day," "Second day," "Third day," and so on. Whether by "day" the narrator of Genesis intended literal days or ages is uncertain. But he stuns us with the recital of God's works. (ACSE, 50)

A photographer who takes poor pictures, even though he is an effective soul-winner, should either take his vocation more seriously, change his business, or at least confine his witness to non-customers! No impressive list of converts will offset a poor work record; one's work ought not to be of such questionable caliber that it disgraces God, discredits one's employer, and affronts society. (ACSE, 70)

Even in Eden the cosmic garden to which God assigned man as its keeper and dresser did not maintain itself. The preservation and enhancement of nature was doubly imperative after it was cursed on man's account. Man's neglect of his cosmic duties seems to provoke nature to strike back in self-defense and in reprisal for being disfigured and exploited, as if to remind fallen man that he has no mandate to manipulate and trample nature. Only by returning to the theological-moral-ecological foundations of biblical theism will man escape the passivism toward nature that characterizes Eastern religions and the naturalistic activism of the West. (GRA VI, 264-65)

The duty of work implies the right to work. A society in which joblessness prevails should consider the provision of constructive work a prime concern. (CMSS, 104)

There should be a job corps in each of the Christian churches, concerned to probe work opportunities for unemployed members. (L)

In commuting between the intimate circle of the family and the larger family of society, employer and employee alike are summoned to use their talents for the good of others. According to the scriptural perspective, work becomes a way-station of spiritual witness and service, a daily-traveled bridge between theology and social ethics. (ACSE, 31)

The church needs to channel informed Christians into the realm of vocation, in law, jurisprudence, political service. (S)

Christianity has undoubtedly given new vigor and dignity to the belittled world of work. . . . Instead of being just a time-consuming routine, a drab monotonous sparring for subsistence devoid of ultimate meaning and laden only with burden and uncertainty, the workaday world was now interpreted as a divinely appointed sphere where man as a worker is ordained to glorify God, and in his name to serve his fellow man. (ACSE, 32)

Work actually reveals one's inner being or character. This fact is as true of a magistrate, a taxi driver, or a typist, as it is of the Creator and Redeemer of the universe. (ACSE, 50-51)

If one is truly a believer, no boss and no machine can pluck him out of Christ's hand and thrust him into a morass of meaninglessness. (ACSE, 59)

WORLD RELIGIONS

Early Christian thinkers did not evade the task of evaluating non-biblical religions and philosophies. They spoke of humanly manufactured gods, of religious absurdities and irrationalities, of all variety of conflicting interpretations of the divine, of myths of dead and reborn divinities, of gods guilty of adultery and theft. Beyond this they witnessed to the sovereignty and grace of the one true and living God revealed supremely in Jesus Christ. (TGC, 181)

American society is being penetrated as never before by alien religious influences that the West unhesitatingly once called pagan. Even witchcraft is practiced much as in pre-Christian societies; demonism and satanic cults are likewise on the increase. Various forms of oriental religions call harried and affluent Westerners to quiet mediation and self-denial. Refugees and immigrants from around the world have given new prominence to assorted religious practices. Mosques, shrines and temples now dot our cities alongside the more traditional worship centers. (TGC, 175)

The notion that God's historical covenants embrace all world religions as part of the church that finds fulfillment in Christ, and that Christ is present in nonbiblical religious history from the beginning, is alien to biblical teaching and arbitrarily correlates religion in general with redemptive religion. The New Testament does indeed represent the whole cosmos and all history as finding its final reconciliation in Christ. But from this emphasis we cannot logically infer that nonbiblical religious writings point to Christ in some hidden way. While God's saving design in the Bible has certain universal implications, it does not welcome the world's works-religions as prefatory to the propitiatory work of the Redeemer. The non-biblical religions and religious writings are not oriented to Christ. (GRA VI, 363-64)

By scripture Hindus mean the Srti ("what is heard") and Smrti ("what is remembered"), not what is God-breathed as a literary phenomenon. . . . One can liken the collection of Hindu sacred writings to the canonical biblical books . . . only by relaxing and accommodating the biblical concept of inspiration. (GRA VI, 361)

The Koran has no doctrine of the final conformity of the people of God to the image of Jesus Christ. But if Jesus is already risen from the dead, as Christianity insists, then he exhibits the humanity approved by God for the eternal future; and if he is ascended, as the Koran concedes, it is he who controls the gates of eternity. If Muhammad is a sinner, he will be judged by Jesus the just and holy Messiah. As it is, Islamic tradition considers Muhammad and other Muslim prophets (Shiites include their imams or leaders) sinless, although the Koran by contrast contains several references to Muhammad's sins. (GRA VI, 503)

Unlike Buddhism, Christianity does not put a premium on self-extinction, nor does it, like Hinduism, treat human life as a mere transmigratory phenomenon, nor is it like much of Islam, in flight from the realities of this world, nor does it protect itself by denying others the right to change their religion. (WT)

WORLD VIEW

The mother who aborts a fetus with a handicap and the mother who showers love on a handicapped child have different world-life views. The mother who abandons an unwanted child has a world view different from the mother who believes no child should be unwanted. The lover who doesn't tell his fiancee that he carries a recessive gene for Tay-Sachs disease or that he has herpes has a world-life view different from the lover who thinks his intended mate ought to know all the risks to which he will expose her. The professor who trades grades for sex has a world-life view different from the professor who thinks all students should be judged by academic standards. (WT)

Many teachers are not secular humanists; some are devout Christians. But the philosophy that more influentially than any other gets through the classroom today is secular humanism: the reduction of reality to space-time processes and events, the transiency of all existence, the relativity of all ideas and ideals to their cultural setting, and man as the definer of truth and the good. (L)

Humanism has penetrated education, the mass media, and politics, and it has debased God by insisting that he is irrelevant to the public realm. (CT2)

The gray mist of secularism stupefies the sense of holiness, stifles moral outrage, intimidates ethical indignation, questions the worth of purity. (CMSS, 40)

What paganism is doing to human life—not only to the life of the spirit but to the whole self and to man in society—demands penetrating analysis. What remains of virtue when the human species is considered animal flesh useful for sexual exploitation, profitable for material gain, serviceable for political terrorism? We discuss nuclear war in terms of anticipated body counts, as if humans were so many cows or horses. What has happened to humaneness in a world where some ten million persons have AIDS and the whole human race is imperiled? (TGC, 174)

The world view of Western secularism and that of Sino-Soviet communism both acquiesce in this dilution of the real world to impersonal processes and events. (GRA I, 135)

While American humanism inconsistently borrows the bare bones of a social ethic from the Judeo-Christian heritage, it ignores the great biblical mandate that man the creature is to love God the creator with his whole being. (CMSS, 13)

The mindset of modernity is but a transitory phenomenon. But it will exploit the illusion of permanence if we do not effectively exhibit its weaknesses and more importantly exhibit the superiority of the theistic view. Modernity is but an agonizing moment in the history of civilizations; only a view that has eternal validity can hope to be forever contemporary. (TGC, 142)

Evangelical colleges fail their constituencies most of all in respect to Christian world-life view fulfillment. To be sure, all evangelical campuses declare their devotion to it, and feature that devotion as one reason why students should enroll. But faculty delineation is often disappointing, and sometimes hardly rises above a devotional level. (TGC, 112)

As never before, humanity is confronted by two world views, two life views, the divergences between which are quite plain in every department of interpretation. They stand so far apart today that each denies the right of the other to life; they are no longer merged in a compromise synthesis which disguises their differences; they have worked themselves out again into first-century contrariety. . . . Between a revelational and a non-revelational system there stands a line that reaches from the Tigris-Euphrates valley to the new heavens and the new earth. (RMM, 237-38)

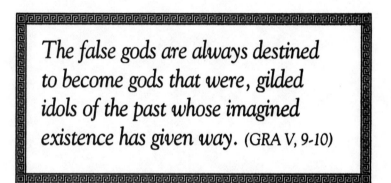

The false gods are always destined to become gods that were, gilded idols of the past whose imagined existence has given way. (GRA V, 9-10)

ABOUT THE AUTHOR

Dr. Carl F. H. Henry has earned a reputation as one of the leading evangelical theologians of this century. Born in New York City in 1913, he received degrees from Wheaton College, North Baptist Theological Seminary, and his Ph.D. from Boston University. He was ordained in 1941 and taught theology at North Baptist Theological Seminary. He then helped to found Fuller Theological Seminary in Pasadena, California, and served on its faculty for nine years.

In 1956, Dr. Henry was one of the founding editors of *Christianity Today*. After twelve years as the magazine's editor, he continued as editor-at-large until 1977. Since then, he has remained busy as an author and lecturer. For many years he was a lecturer-at-large for World Vision, and presently he serves in the same capacity for Prison Fellowship.

The publication of *Carl Henry at His Best* marks his thirty-third published book since 1941. Among his works are *Twilight of a Great Civilization, Christian Countermoves in a Decadent Culture, The Christian Mindset in a Secular Society, Confessions of a Theologian*, and the six-volumes of *God, Revelation and Authority*.